This book is dedicated to my wonderful far-flung family:
Jared, Jodi, Chris, Sebastien, Mika, and Bodi (the dog),
and to the social media & networking platforms that allow us to
communicate and keep close.

Acknowledgements

I would like to acknowledge the thought leadership and great work of the following social media Gurus, whose knowledge and brains I have found so important in my struggle to learn these new media. For those many leaders I have missed listing, forgive me.

Advertising Age	adage.com
Tom Anderson, Anderson Analytics	andersonanalystics.com
Jono Bacon, The Art of Community (book)	artofcommunityonline.org
Perry Belcher	perrybelcher.com
Boetcher Duggan & White	fullcirc.com
Peter Block, Community (Book)	amazon.com
Chris Brogan	chrisbrogan.com
CMB Consumer Pulse	blog.cmbinfo.com
Jonathan Carson, the Nielsen Company	en-us.nielsen.com
Lon S. Cohen	lonscohen.com/blog
Clark Fredrickson, e-Marketer Daily	emarketer.com
Bill Geist	billgeist.typepad.com
Steve Glauberman	imediaconnection.com
Hubspot	hubspot.com
Mark Hughes, Buzzmarketing (book)	buzzmarketing.com
Mitch Joel	twistimage.com/blog
Cindy King	cindyking.biz
Frederic Lardinois	readwriteweb.com
Pam Lontos	prpr.net/
David Meerman-Scott	webinknow.com
Jacob Morgan	successful-blog.com
Amber Nashland	brasstackthinking.com
Sarah Needleman	muckrack.com /sarahneedleman
Dr. Jacob Nielsen	http://www.useit.com
Amy Porterfield	amyporterfield.com
PRWeb	prweb.com
Leise Reichelt	disambiguity.com

Lon Safko and David Brake	thesocialmediabible.com
Marie Smith	marismith.com
Mike Stelzner, Social Media Examiner	examiner.com
Liz Strauss	successful-blog.com
Troy Thompson	travel2dot0.com

A special thanks to **eMarketer** for the use of many of their excellent graphs and charts.

eMarketer.

This book could not have been published without the hard work of editors: Curtis Wright and Pamela Moeller and designer Terry Thayer.

Table of Contents
Secrets for Successful Social Media Marketing

PREFACE

John Hope-Johnstone

Hi, social media is just one part of an overall customer experience. Social media does not have its own galaxy, so ask:

> "What can we learn from social media that can be spread across all other areas of marketing? What can we learn to make our customer's experience more enjoyable, our product or service more accessible and, ultimately, more sales oriented?" Chris Brogan, http://www.chrisbrogan.com

A good social media strategy will extract insights from various social media platforms and leverage them to help improve both your own strategic view and the strategic plan for your business. Your social media can and should help your business grow in the following areas:

- Better public relations

- Brand image

- Brand awareness

- Lead generation

- Knowledge leadership in your field

- Customer education

- Finding new customers

- Improving internal corporate communications

- Increasing buzz about your product

- Building social and political capital (remember it is part of public relations)

This book contains five key secrets and many more tips that will drive your social media success.

Enjoy!

Note: Because Social Media and Internet Marketing are moving at light speed, some of the URLs listed in this book may be out of date by the time you purchase. Please know that all URLs were tested prior to publication. Please accept out apologies for any links that might have stopped working.

Introduction:

Marketing is in the greatest period of flux in its history, with a bewildering array of marketing channels, programs, and platforms for you to use.

I understand how complex marketing is these days. I coach brands on Internet and Social Media Marketing. I do this through speeches, full- and half-day seminars, and working one on one. Everything I teach is designed to create a closer relationship with clients and their prospects.

This work has led me to discover five key secrets about social media. I believe that these secrets are invaluable for every brand marketer.

This book looks at social media from a marketing perspective, as do our seminars. At **HPR** (www.johnhopejohnstone.com) we are **marketers first** and social media is just one of the marketing tools we use. This book is a compilation and an update of my many blog posts on the subject, with new additions. Follow the blog at www.buzzmaster.wordpress.com for more insights into social media.

We firmly believe that social media falls under the marketing discipline of public relations. Of all marketing activities, public relations seem to be the vaguest but it has also become one of the most important marketing tools of the twenty-first century. Therefore, to understand more about social media we must first learn more about public relations.

The Tao of Public relations is the belief that any third party reference has a far more positive impact on your brand than your own words. "Buzz" is the most powerful marketing tool in today's marketing arsenal. The results of good public relations are far more valuable to you captured than left alone. So, reprint that article! Quote that blog! Redistribute that YouTube video! Save and re-Tweet that complimentary Tweet-then your hard work lives on forever.

People will patronize your organization because of its perceived image. Your corporate brand is partly created by the brand's physical appearance (design), but also by how people in your target audience **feel** about it. It's similar to how your personal image is created by a combination of what you wear, what you say, what you write, the good works you do, and by rumors that are spread about you. Social media can be a powerful tool in creating a strong, positive brand image.

In the twenty-first century, the level of trust in anything corporate has decreased steadily over the years. The buzzword of today is "authenticity." The more we have experienced life, the more cautious we become regarding the authenticity of the next experience. Only third party references can increase our faith in a product. Social media can provide those third party references and hence develop a level of trust.

Social media and social networking create **"social validation."**

"Social validation, or social proofing, is a psychological phenomenon that occurs in ambiguous situations when people do not have enough information to make opinions independently and instead look for external clues such as: consumer comments, popularity, star ratings and third party endorsements from friends and family to help develop that level of trust." Wikipedia

The official definition of public relations adopted by the Canadian Public relations Society in June of 2009 is:

> *"Public Relations are (yes they are plural) the strategic management of relationships between an organization and its diverse publics, through the use of communication, to achieve mutual understanding, realize organizational goals, and serve the public interest."* (Flynn, Gregory and Valin, 2008)

Public Relations have also been defined as:

> *"The collective effort of any group to win the understanding and esteem of people, by its conduct deserve that esteem, and by its communications to maintain it."*
> "How to Market Tourism in the 21st Century" by John Hope-Johnstone

These definitions seem to indicate that social media should fall under the marketing plan heading of public relations.

However, it does not mean that social media efforts or public relations should be housed exclusively in any one department of any organization. It becomes the collective effort of everybody involved in the organization to win the understanding and esteem of its customers. In social media, we must win the understanding of our communities of common interest for what we are trying to accomplish, and by our conduct, as exposed in our social media, deserve their esteem.

When we speak about public relations and social media, we must not confuse the words "brand image" with a false facade. Our image and our actual behavior must be one and the same. Our image must be accurate. If it is not, we will soon be found out.

Secret Number One:

Ask One Simple Question before You Begin!

> *The question is: WHY?*
> *Just because the technology exists does not mean you have to use it. I expect your business or organization has been getting along quite well without social media. Before you go any further, answer the question: Why am I getting into social media and adding more work?*

Once you have answered the KEY question "Why"; ask the following four questions and if the answers are positive, you are ready to enter the forbidden Kingdom of social media.

1. Are my consumers even involved in this social media thing?

2. If the present generation of consumer is not involved in social media, is the next?

3. Is social media of interest to me personally?

4. Am I involved at this present time, in social media?

If, after answering these questions, you aren't rushing to the store to get your money back on this book, then we are ready to go ahead a bit further. Let's look closer into the big "why" by dipping one toe into the social media swimming pool and check out the social media landscape.

a. The Social Media Landscape

What is Social Media?

> Social media is the content; it's the writing, pictures, reviews, or videos that are placed on the Internet for interactive purposes. "Media is the intersection between technology and content." Robert Iger, CEO Disney Corp.

What is Social Networking?

> Social networking via the Internet is the connection that happens between people reading and viewing social media. The world famous sales guru Zig Ziglar once said, "Networking is getting what YOU want by helping other people get what THEY want." I have always held this to be true and it has never let me down.

I am going to categorize some of the 9 profiles of people creating social media content, or engaged in social networking.

The different types of motivation people have in joining social media platforms, (brand promotion aside), are:

1. **Friendlies**: People keeping up with far-flung friends

2. **Lonelies**: People looking for new friends

3. **Slaves**: Employees expanding their careers or looking for work

4. **Groupies**: People following people they like or admire

5. **Famers**: Building a large following on social media

6. **Sharers**: Sharing content, pictures, and videos just for the enjoyment of sharing

7. **Critics**: Either positive or negative comments on consumer content-driven sites such as TripAdvisor, Yelp, FourSquare, etc.

8. **Gamers**: Much neglected, but a large social activity of gaming against world-wide opponents

9. **Players**: Businesses growing their customer channels and prospecting

People can be in more than one of the above categories and change from one day to the next. But whatever our mood of the day, we need to be spoken to in a different voice depending on if we happen to be looking for new friends, a new business contact, or reaching out to someone we just met.

All of these folks divide into three major categories:

1. Avid content creators

2. Avid content consumers

3. A bit of both

Leisa Reichelt says that the updates we share publicly with friends and followers in Twitter (and blogs and Flickr....) add up to what she calls "ambient intimacy."

> *"Ambient intimacy is being able to keep in touch with people with a level of regularity and intimacy that you wouldn't usually have access to, because time and space conspire to make it impossible. Flickr lets us see what friends are eating for lunch, how they have redecorated their bedroom, their latest haircut. Twitter tells me when they are hungry, what technology is currently frustrating them, who they are having drinks with tonight"* Leisa Reichelt,
> (http://www.disambiguity.com/ambient-intimacy/.

b: Making Your Organization More Human

I was giving a social media seminar to my good friends at Travel and Tourism Research Association's Greater Western Chapter in Montana when it struck me that one of the driving forces behind the growth of social media for brand promotion purposes is the demand by the consumer to make corporate America more credible and human.

Organizations of all sizes must understand that in the twenty-first century, consumers are demanding transparency, credibility and a human face to business. The chart on the next page shows that a motivated purchaser will trust reviews from fellow consumers, before anyone else:

Most Credible Source for Information About a Brand on a Social Networking Site According to Internet Users Worldwide, January 2010 (% of respondents)

A consumer	38%
The brand itself	32%
A journalist	7%
A marketer	3%
Another brand	1%

Note: n=2,065
Source: InSites Consulting, "Social Media Around the World," March 22, 2010

113535   www.eMarketer.com

In discussing with business owners the concept of increasing credibility by providing a human face for their brand, some have expressed a concern about having just ONE face humanize a company.

They are concerned the face might leave the organization (or the Earth), then what happens to the brand? They are also concerned that 50% might trust the face and 50% might not. These are very legitimate concerns.

However, in researching the same question with social media consumers, they *don't* actually want just one face or one spokesperson to help make the brand more human. They are actually much happier to get to know many of the company's faces. "We like to do business with people we like," they told me. "It builds trust."

The other side of the coin from trust is transparency. Businesses need to speak in a way that today's consumers understand and not in a way that some lawyer or marketing professional feels they should speak.

If a company accepts this philosophy of exposing its human face and being as transparent as possible, then the next step is to figure out how to take the company's **brand promise** and translate it into a message about which there can be a conversation on social media.

The social media conversation could be about a socially responsible act, a staff member volunteering for a good cause, or a marketing promotion.

Using public relations and the medium of social media, you can start a buzz going and hold a conversation. Social media can report on the success of a public relations activity, give visuals, and show purpose as they relate to the brand promise.

While corporations (mostly small- and medium-sized) have done a great job of joining the social media conversation, there is a vague sense in some quarters that social media is not producing the returns expected.

To answer that concern I have to remind people that social media platforms were not developed as marketing tools, they were **adopted!** They were created to facilitate social interaction. So if businesses wish to have a conversation with their customers it is available to them to do so.

Using social media as a tool to grant customers a platform to gush with admiration or vent anger towards a brand is not enough. For many companies, the **wall** of the brand is still separating the consumer from the human side of the brand, just as the curtain separated Dorothy from the Wizard in *The Wizard of Oz*.

My friend Troy Thompson (http://travel2dot0.com/) expands on the concept that employees ARE your brand in an excellent Travel 2.0 blog post. In his blog, Thompson argues that employees ARE a major part of your brand, and that corporate culture is an important part of the brand image. Public perception of your company IS your brand, and a logo or a made-up tag line is not a complete representation.

He argues that it is your employees that set the tone of your brand, even with the polished and scheduled messages from your "official" fan pages.

Troy states that people want to connect with other people via social media, not brands or an agency-created persona.

The people in your organization are, (hopefully), passionate about their jobs and active on social media.

If a corporation has enthusiastic brand angels within their employees who believe in its product or service and believe in the ethics, which the company upholds, then I, for one, would want to check out that brand's products or services.

We forget that technology is benign and that a megaphone with no voice shouting through it is silent and useless. A phone with no one at the other end is of no value. All technology can do for us is enable us to communicate. WHAT we communicate will signal our success or failure, NOT the technology.

> **Social media is NOT an answer; it is an enabler. It enables communities of common interest to find each other and have a conversation. Social media can be a great enabler for corporations to show their human face and to be transparent. If that is deemed to be of value to the organization then it should be used; if it's not, then leave it alone.** Quoted from www.buzzmaster.wordpress.com and slightly altered and expanded from Robert Abate, http://www.information-management.com/blog/robert_abate.html. June 8, 2009.

c: The Importance of Your Social Media Presence

In this section I am paraphrasing from one of my favorite bloggers on the new media, Mitch Joel (http://www.twistimage.com/blog/), from his blog regarding "The New Marketing Conversation." (By the way if you haven't read his book, *Six Pixels of Separation,* do so quickly: http://www.amazon.com/Six-Pixels-Separation-Connected-ebook/dp/B002M2AT2I).

In the blog, he emphasizes that the discipline of marketing is once again changing as we morph to being publishers of worthwhile, authentic and valuable content.

Today, it is our corporate "back story" explaining the history of our product or service, and our philosophy and ethics that differentiates us from all the noise of our competition. As our Web sites become more and more complex it becomes clear that the "mother ship," our Web site, is no longer the only important Web presence we own. What IS now important is your total SEARCH PRESENCE.

When someone searches for your product or service and your Web site comes up on the search results page (SRP), that's nice. If your brand's Web site comes up along with your blogs, Facebook, Twitter, LinkedIn, videos, podcasts, and Flickr, with well-written meta descriptions, then you begin to have a critical mass of Web presence. That is important in the eyes of the consumer because the more exposure on the SRP the more important you are presumed to be.

Below is the SRP of my Web presence. Notice that it contains the Web site, Twitter, Facebook, the blog, and the meta- descriptions. Even though a search of my name is obviously going to produce good results, it is still important that I have critical mass and presence:

About **John Hope-Johnstone** ☆
About HPR and **John Hope-Johnstone**, social media
www.**johnhopejohnstone**.com/about.htm - Cached
➕ Show more results from johnhopejohnstone.com

John Hope-Johnstone | Facebook ☆
Friends: Laima Vaseris, Irene Zenev, Dan Shryock, Kate
John Hope-Johnstone is on Facebook. Join Faceboo
and others you may know. Facebook gives people the p
www.facebook.com/**hopejohnstone** - Cached - Similar

Buzz Master's Blog | Thoughts and Ideas on
John Hope-Johnstone. Bon jour, I have been a very ba
Buenos tardes, in this post I want to give some thought ...
buzzmaster.wordpress.com/ - Cached

John Hope-Johnstone (HopeJohnstone) or
Great to meet you! I'm a father, traveler, lover of life, & CI
link above and let's join up on facebook as well.
twitter.com/**hopejohnstone** - Cached - Similar

By 2011, it is widely assumed that Google will rank the search results page (SRP) not only by context and authority of your Web site, but also by a personalization algorithm that will include social media and personal information as shown in the following information from Hubspot.com:

Time Period	Algorithm
Before 2000	Web page Content (contextual)
2000-2010	Context + Authority (inbound links)
2011 +	Context + Authority + Social Media ranking

> Your presence has more to do with good content than your marketing pitch. As **Mitch Joel** explains, a problem arises if you don't understand the differences between "marketing" and "publishing." Mitch Joel: http://www.twistimage.com/blog/archives/the-new-marketing-conversation/:

Marketing is about:

- "Figuring out what to produce, how to price it, distribute it, and how to tell people about it.
- Selling something.
- Getting people to believe in what you're selling.
- Building a brand.
- Building loyalty.

- Creating word of mouth.
- Positioning your brand in people's minds.

Publishing is about:

- The production and dissemination of information.
- Creating a unique perspective and sharing it with a broader audience.
- Distributing ideas.
- Offering a new/different perspective.
- Making something of value available for the public to view."

As Mitch says, marketing and publishing are dramatically different. They both require very different skill sets and very different philosophies, yet both are equally important in the twenty-first century.

Marketing has become far more than writing good brochure or advertising copy, although that's still very important. It is differentiating your product through valuable online content.

The Internet was originally designed for the efficient flow of data and information, and it continues to be so. So, create good, valuable content!

d: The Difference Between Social Networking and Broadcasting

You probably have been networking all your life. We join civic clubs, Rotary, Zonta, etc. All the Internet has done is added to these excellent networking venues and placed them on **steroids**.

When does social networking become broadcasting? Celebrities Ashton Kutcher and Ellen DeGeneres together have more Twitter followers than the populations of Ireland, Norway, and Panama! (http://socialnomics.net/tag/social-media-video/).

It must be very difficult to "network" with that number of people. I think it is very impressive, and I am very jealous, but it is important to understand that when microblogs reach this number of followers, they become a "broadcasting" tool, which is used primarily to point the way to additional subject matter.

I tend to value re-tweets more than obtaining large numbers of people, most of whom I don't really know. What I broadcast (usually) is a link to my blog, or my Facebook fan page, or my Web site. Places where I can help people find information they want, and start a deeper relationship. We have developed a network of re-tweeters who are followers that have agreed to re-tweet and spread each other's word. We also use lists and hash tags as much as possible.

Here is an article I found on the Portland Examiner Web site by Mike Stelzner, founder of Social Media Examiner, regarding networking and broadcasting (http://www.examiner.com). In the article he quotes Lon S. Cohen, http://lonscohen.com/blog/, as saying:

"Social Media can be called a strategy and an outlet for broadcasting, while Social Networking is a tool and a utility for connecting with others.

The difference is not just semantics but in the features and functions put into these websites by their creators which dictates the way they are to be used. There's also a kind of, which came first, the chicken or the egg kind of argument to be made here. I suspect that Social Networking came first which evolved into Social Media."

Stelzner further distinguishes which platforms fall into which category: LinkedIn, he says, falls more under social networking, whereas YouTube is more social media. What about Facebook?

> **"Facebook is a Web 3.0 platform with the whole package. It straddles the Social Media and Social Networking divide perfectly."**
> **Hence, its dominance in the field.** (Quoted from:
> http://lonscohen.com/blog/2009/04/difference-between-social-media-and-social-networking/)

Still confused? Stelzner continues to say that there's perhaps a simpler way to process the divide. Social media platforms are tools for sharing and discussing information. Social networking is the use of communities of interest to connect to others. You can use social media to facilitate social networking. Alternatively, you can network by leveraging social media. If you're still scratching your head, be sure to watch this terrific Social Networking 101 video: http://www.youtube.com/watch?v=6a_KF7TYKVc. Don't be daunted, because knowing the Web, I'm certain we'll be wrestling with new terminology soon.

e) How to Promote Through Social Media

As I mentioned earlier in the book, the microblogs tell people "who you are," and they often point towards more information with a URL. The macroblogs tell people "what you know" and confirm that you are a thought leader on your subject. Your Web site (the mother ship) tells people "what you do."

Once these interlinking platforms have been populated with great content, the question becomes, "Which part of your organization can be best served by social media?"

To help answer this question, it is interesting to look at how marketing executives are measuring social media return on investment (ROI) in their companies. This does not mean that they are necessarily measuring it correctly, but it is indicative of how the marketing community is using the role of social media at this moment in time. The following chart, found on eMarketing.com, shows how executives are spending their time and money on social media:

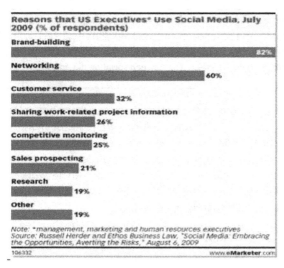

Reasons that US Executives* Use Social Media, July 2009 (% of respondents)

Brand-building — 82%
Networking — 60%
Customer service — 32%
Sharing work-related project information — 26%
Competitive monitoring — 25%
Sales prospecting — 21%
Research — 19%
Other — 19%

Note: *management, marketing and human resources executives
Source: Russell Herder and Ethos Business Law, "Social Media: Embracing the Opportunities, Averting the Risks," August 6, 2009
106332   www.eMarketer.com

Brand building seems to be the major activity at 82%. I interpret this as building your reputation, which, as I have already said in this book should fall under the auspices of the public relations department.

> In my book *How to Market Tourism in the 21st Century* (2009), I define Public relations as, "The development of social, political and market capital through third party endorsement. The value of Public relations lies in capturing and reproducing it so it lives forever!"

One of the "publics" contained in Public relations is "community relations," or showing the community that your organization is a giving contributor. "Community" can also mean your virtual communities as well as your real communities. Any civic good deed or charity you have supported, along with fund raising activities and actions that follow, are all good content to shout-out about on social media. The path can go from a Twitter shout-out with a tiny URL to a Facebook "event" invitation where people show their support. This then points to a short blog or vlog that explains the activity and purpose in detail. A vlog can also contain volunteers making comments or an after-the-fact video clip of the event.

Comments, retweets, blogs, and press articles should be captured and reproduced, (with permission), so that the social capital they build can live on in your Web site. Snap shots of good Tweets, and comments on blogs and other social media platforms, can be placed on the brand's Web site promoting the growth of social capital, which is one of the main purposes of social media.

Networking is the second-most-valued activity listed on the above chart at 60%. If, as Zig Ziglar said, networking is "getting what you want by helping others get what they want," then how can social media help? Networking provides gains in the second part of my definition of Public relations, and that is growing "political capital."

You gain political capital by helping others get what THEY want. This can be achieved by aiming them towards the information desired, or by providing an introduction to another mentor or individual that can help them further. LinkedIn and Facebook are both great sites for mentoring. Whatever you are doing in social media, the bigger question is, do you have the staff time to do a good job?

f) Finding the Time for Social Media

I spend quite a bit of time giving seminars on social media and social networking. It's my thing! The comment I hear more than any other from my audience is, "I just don't have the time for social media."

The initial time you spend on figuring out the social media is not excessive, but the amount of time it takes in maintaining them with powerful content, and growing your reach, is substantial.

As an example, it took me only a few minutes when I first opened my WordPress blog account, but I have spent countless hours on Sundays (my usual writing day) cursing and swearing over my blog prose. Another key factor is that the more effort you put into social media, the more you will get out. It is as simple as that, as the following chart clearly shows:

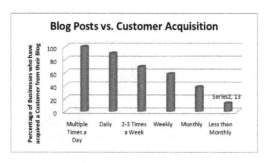

The above chart with statistics from HubSpot.com, states that 100% of bloggers surveyed who posted more than once daily acquire customers from their blogs. These are obviously serious and good bloggers, and deserve to acquire clients from their blogs. However, this is also a serious time commitment.

Here are some initial time management questions to ask yourself as you launch into social media adventure, (adapted from Amber Nashland's article found at http://www.brasstackthinking.com):

1) Realistically, how many staff hours can your organization spend on social media each day? Do you have resources/people other than yourself? What can you realistically expect of your staff or yourself? (Note: if you're serious about doing social media, you need to find roughly an hour a day to start with, at least.)

2) Which two or three social networking platforms make the best sense for you to start with based on your listening efforts so far? What are your goals for social media on those sites? What are the cultures of those communities and how will your participation align with those cultures?

3) Have you evaluated your current online and offline Public relations efforts, to determine what's working and what you might supplement or replace with social media?

We have kept **time diaries** for our clients as they started out on their social media journeys. Based on that, I'm giving you are my estimates of the time required to promote your brand on social media. I am going to use the term "staff hours" because it does NOT mean that YOU personally have to contribute all these hours. You can delegate, or you can request "guest" content providers, (as long as you indicate, a guest has written the posting):

3 to 4 staff hours per workweek: If you have three to four hours each week, then you have enough hours to look, listen, and learn. Begin by researching which social media platforms the majority of your clients are presently using. Open up Twitter and Facebook accounts and any other social media platforms your consumer research shows to be interesting. Get involved by dipping your toes in the water.

5 to 6 staff hours per workweek: If you have five to six hours each week then your organization can start becoming involved. By "becoming involved" I mean begin to build followers and friends, and possibly add a short weekly blog or vlog. Now you are becoming a "minimal content provider."

7 to 10 staff hours per workweek: With two hours per workday, your organization is becoming more engaged in social media, and someone most likely needs to be appointed as a "Community Manager." You are now becoming involved in providing **effective** social media content.

11 to 20 staff hours per workweek: With roughly two to three hours per workday, your organization is becoming a driving force in social media and is providing a significant social media presence, and you may need to assign a "Social Media Manager" to help your community managers and brand angels do their work.

Here are some other ways you can improve your time and personnel costs on social media and still get great returns:

1. Don't operate without a social media strategy (it's a waste of time).

2. Make sure that your strategy has effective metrics of success and failure.

3. Make sure the strategy has an editorial calendar to guide your writing and content.

4. Unless you are only into broadcasting, use quality not quantity followers. (Both are great if you can handle it, but it is very difficult.)

5. Develop a key influencer list (you most likely already have one).

One time saver that is being touted by some social media gurus is to connect your social media platforms so that your information goes out on one social media platform (such as Facebook) but appears on all your profiles (such as Twitter and LinkedIn); I call this "cross-blasting".

I am not a big fan of cross-blasting social media content. The reason behind this testiness is that research has shown that each platform attracts different psychographic profiles and communities, and I believe that the message has to be tuned for each. Now, if time is *so* important, then use the button that says, "blast this out to every platform" with my blessing but I think you are losing the opportunity to tailor the message to the audience.

> Don't forget that blasting a message out just once is never going to reach all your social media followers. Do it at least five times over a week at different times of the day and with different wording but the same basic message and URL.

g) Developing a Community with Social Media

Today in marketing, we speak less about demographics and psychographics, and more about "communities". Communities have a common interest, and that interest is usually coalesced by the search function:

> "A community is fundamentally an interdependent human system given form by the conversation it holds within itself." (Peter Block, *Community: The Structure of Belonging,* 2008. http://www.amazon.com/Community-Structure-Belonging-Peter-Block/dp/1576754871)

In the past, the term community related to platforms such as forums and message boards. However, with the rise of social media platforms such as Facebook, Twitter, LinkedIn, Yelp, and many others, the term community has become vague and more loosely defined. These communities may exist only for a nanosecond, or may continue for many years.

We have two choices to build our communities: 1) Join an already established community (this is what we usually do); or 2) Create our own community, around either a common interest or the sharing of a particular bit of knowledge.

Today, we often speak about "virtual communities" which exist primarily for the sharing of knowledge. Sir Tim Berners-Lee created the World Wide Web for the purpose of the dissemination of knowledge, and the majority of the communities gather around a desire to discuss a particular subject. New knowledge keeps the community growing and stable. The community must be continuously fed like a hungry beast with fresh pieces of knowledge.

Here are some of the types of "community" that people have enjoyed through these online connections, (written by Sue Boetcher, Heather Duggan, and Nancy White at: www.fullcirc.com).

- **Socialize** – Meeting people, playing around, sharing jokes and stories, and just taking interest in each other. Communities like this often focus around bulletin boards and chat rooms or social media sites such as facebook. An example of such a community is Electric Minds at http://www.electricminds.org.

- **Work together** (business) – Distributed work groups within and between companies use online community to build their team, keep in touch, and even work on projects together. A very detailed description of how online work groups work can be found at http://www.awaken.com and http://www.bigbangworkshops.com.

- **Work together** (geography and interests) – Freenets (see the Freenet Directory, http://www.freenetdirectory.com/) have offered local communities ways to communicate and work together. Community groups such as soccer teams, school groups, and others have used online Freenet community to provide forums for information and discussion, helping bring groups together.

- **Work together** (issues) – Virtual communities have been very important to people who share interests in issues and causes. Support groups for people dealing with certain diseases, causes such as politics or the environment, or people studying together, all can form a nucleus for an online community.

- **Have topical conversations** – Online salons and discussion forums such as The Well (http://www.well.com), Salon's Table Talk (as of mid-2001 a paid subscription model) (http://www.salon.com), Cafe Utne (http://www.utne.com), and others have formed communities of people who enjoy conversations about topics and shared interests. Forum One (http://www.forumone.com/) noted in 1999 that the top seven topics for forums registered at their site are around the following topics: (Next page).

1. Relationships (16%)

2. Business and finance (8%),

3. Health (5%)

4. Hobbies (4%)

5. Religion (3%)

6. Music (3%)

7. International understanding (3%).

Writing this book gave me pause to think about the communities in which I am involved. I don't belong to any bulletin boards, but I am involved with industry forums and social media and social networking platforms. Here are some social media that I believe still should hold the title of Community:

1. Those who regularly follow my blog could be called a community (poor things).

2. The LinkedIn groups that I belong to and those whose brains I pick religiously are a community.

3. Although random, my Facebook friends are a community.

4. Twitter's hash tags are free-flowing communities exchanging knowledge about their fields of social media. They ebb and flow, but nonetheless are a community. They can be considered a community, but mostly they are broadcasting and pointing to additional sources of rich media on the subject.

5. I subscribe to various knowledge e-zines. I suppose all of my fellow subscribers are part of a community, and we are asked to comment on the e-zine. It is a rag-tag form of a community, but a community nonetheless.

> **The key to forming a community lies in developing a sense of "belonging" according to Jono Bacon, author of the book *The Art of Community: Building the New Age of Participation*: "Part of that sense of belonging has to do with getting a tangible 'reward' from the community. That reward can be entertainment, knowledge, friendship, support, or even financial gain." Jono Bacon, http://www.artofcommunityonline.org/**

Communities are incredibly ethereal, and tend to come and go at will. I believe that to try and overly structure them is a recipe for disaster; just let them be. Feed them and nourish them with knowledge, but don't try to control and over-structure them.

For the majority of us, we are going to find our community within the 800-pound-gorillas of social media, such as Facebook, LinkedIn, and Twitter. We tend to treat these communities rather casually, but with a small amount of effort they can be powerful building tools for success.

> **Two key elements to building your social media communities often forgotten are: 1) Build it with people who are key influencers in your world and 2) Be social: Introduce people, mentor people, and help people get where they want to go. By doing this, you will build your own reputation and your community will prosper.**

Whichever communities or platforms you use in social media, remember **they do NOT stand alone**, as you will find out in the following, secret number two.

Secret Two:

Social Media Platforms do NOT Stand Alone!

a: How Social Media Platforms Tie Together to Build Awareness

So, now you have acquired a Twitter account and a Facebook fan page for your organization. Your Community Managers are being busy little bees tweeting and writing blogs. You are posting videos on your YouTube channel and photos of your publicity events on Flickr, but...no one knows about it!

> The first rule to improving your social media marketing is an understanding that each platform needs to cross promote. No platform stands alone. They all must eventually drive the participant to your Web site and a greater understanding of your brand.

To quote Steve Glauberman's article of June 12, 2009, in one of my favorite Web sites, http://www.imediaconnection.com:

"Social media has been embraced by businesses big and small, and that's both promising and commendable. As you continue to invest in fleshing out these initiatives, though, keep the importance of cross promoting them in mind.

Consider your cross-media marketing campaigns as a whole, and look for ways each channel could potentially accommodate advertising for your social efforts. Increasing your visibility directly increases the number of current and potential customers who choose to maintain an ongoing social dialogue with your company and brand."

> **Over 40% of people fail to achieve their brand potential in social media because they have no clear-cut strategy.**

Our strategy at **HPR** is that we want our Web site, www.johnhopejohnstone.com, to be where people end up. So the microblogs like Twitter and social media platforms such as Facebook, MySpace, etc., point to the macroblog (real blogs) which in our case is www.buzzmaster.wordpress.com. It in turn points to my Web site.

Therefore, my micro-blogs on Twitter point to our original content on our macro-blog, which then points to my Web site, http://www.johnhopejohnstone.com.

In reality, they all point to each other because in the real world people enter and exit from many different directions as the slide on the next page depicts.

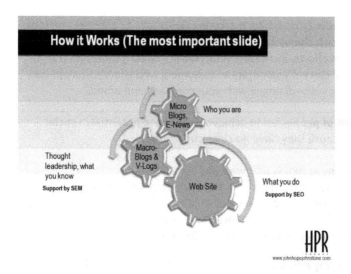

Our Web site analytics show that my crazy dreams quite often actually come true. The top referrer to my Web site is nearly always facebook, second is my blog, search is number three and Twitter and Linkedin are four and five.

Cross promotion is vitally important as no platform stands alone! Each platform provides a deeper understanding by the public regarding your brand.

To promote your Facebook business page, grab an Official Badge from Facebook to incorporate onto your Web site. Don't forget that your e-newsletters can deliver your social media to an audience that has already indicated they want to get to know you better by opting-in.

All these actions to market your media content are speaking to the converted. What about those who have **never heard about you?** Here we need to add a strategy involving search engine marketing (SEM) and search engine optimization (SEO).

I am a big believer in making sure that the topics of my postings are popular and being searched a lot (no brain trust there). Now, it's a bit easier for me because I write about social media and, currently, it's a very popular topic.

My next step is to make sure that the title and keywords I am using are those that many people are using in their searches. To find out how many people have searched your topic on the search engines, you can pay some money and get some nice little bells and whistles from http://www.wordtracker.com, or get the basics free from Google at: https://adwords.google.com/select/KeywordToolExternal, which basically tells you how many people have used the keyword or key phrases.

If you don't have an idea what to write about (poor you), you can get all the hot topics from http://www.alltop.com (all the top stories) or the hottest stories on the Internet http://www.popurls.com or http://www.digg.com (best stories). These three Web sites can give you clues to developing popular new content for your blogs or Tweets or Facebook posts that will grow your readership because the topics are high on the search engine popularity charts at that moment.

Remember, make sure you are writing about a topic in which people have an interest. It is a wonderful world where you can actually check this out using Wordtracker or Web CEO or Google to find the number of searches that have taken place using your title.

Now that you have refined your topic and title of your blog or Facebook message, or even your tweet, you need to create a Google Ad Words or/and a Yahoo pay per click campaign. You will only spend money for actual clicks through to your blog or your video channel.

Does it work? Well, here is a good example of the analytics for my blog, http://www.buzzmaster.wordpress.com. You can see that I opened a Pay Per Click campaign (PPC) around September 1, 2009, and then again at the end of the month.

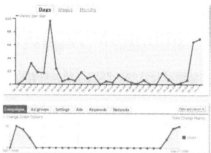
Pay Per Click Campaign

Notice that my readership, which usually plugs along at about 20-30 readers a day (and I am quite happy with that), suddenly zooms to 60-100 readers a day when I turn on the PPC campaign.

With the right advertisement, written correctly, and with search words that are popular in the search engines, wonderful things happen to my blog readership.

b: Facebook Users: What do they look like?

Although the following study is not specific to Facebook it does have key insights into social media users that also hold true for Facebook users.

A 2009 *Ad Age* article reported the results of a new study by Anderson Analytics http://www.andersonanalytics.com. Ad Age reports the study as saying, how you engage in social media and which social platforms you choose say a lot about you.

The Anderson survey studied the demographics and psychographics of both social networkers and non-users, and found that "there are definite data-driven segments in the social-networking-site market," according to Tom Anderson, founder and managing partner of Anderson Analytics.

Tom Anderson reports that the average social networker goes to social sites five days a week and checks in about four times a day for a total of an hour each day. A super-connected group (9%) stays logged in all day and are "constantly checking out what's new."

The report says that feelings about "brands" by people engaged in social networking online are more positive than researchers thought they would be. Some 52% of social networkers had befriended or become a fan of at least one brand. When asked if seeing a brand on a social network makes them feel positive or negative about that brand, an almost-equal 17% said positive and 19% said negative. The other 64% were neutral or didn't care. When asked if they would like more communications from brands, 45% were neutral, while 20% said yes and 35% said no.

Social Network Users Overall:
Social networkers get a bad rap for using social media to pump up their egos and reputations with "fake" friends. The truth is, in general, they're not super-aggressive about building networks. Almost half (45%) said they will link only to family and friends, and another 18% will link only to people they've met in person. That means almost two-thirds associate only with people they know offline. However, the fake-frienders segment are outlanders with 10% of those surveyed saying that they would connect with anyone who is willing to connect with them.

Most users, according to Anderson, are not wasting company time. Only 15% said they go on social networks for personal use at work. (Of course they do, hmmm?)

The report states that social media users' top three interests are:

1. Music

2. Movies

3. Hanging out with friends

They use social media mostly to stay in touch with friends, family, and classmates. Not surprisingly, they do more online than non-users of social media, everything from watching videos to reading blogs to making purchases. They are four times more vocal than non-users when it comes to commenting on discussion boards, posting blog entries, and uploading videos.

Anderson's research breaks down social media users into four categories:

1) Business users

2) Fun seekers

3) Social media mavens

4) Late followers

Of those four, "social media mavens" are the key group. Not only because of their high incomes and decision-making power at companies, but, also because their large social media footprints can make them brand allies and evangelists, Anderson reported. Fun seekers are also an important group because they are the up-and-coming mavens as they transition from students to employees.

Contrary to what some might think, the "late followers" and people who spurn social media aren't tech haters. In fact, they spend as much time as social media fans surfing the web. However, the Anderson study states that they don't use social media for three basic reasons:

1) They don't have the time; 2) They don't think it's secure; or 3) They think it's stupid. While the first two groups — which Anderson labels "time-starved" and "concerned" — may be swayed to join eventually, don't hold out much hope for the last group: 94% said they will never use social media.

Ad Age reports the Anderson study as saying that about 22% of time-starved people said they'll be using social media within three months, and another 27% said they probably would within a year — (when they get the time that is). They're more interested than all others are in other pursuits such as exercise, entertaining, music, and movies.

The concerned non-users are an older demographic (one-third are retired) who don't use social networks because they are worried about their privacy. However, they do recognize value in social media and may join as they become more comfortable with it. In more recent studies the new and early retirement group is changing this demographic and becoming one of the fastest groups to become late adopters into social media.

Social media non-users in general don't shop online as much as social networkers, but they are much more likely to visit online retailers Amazon and eBay.

There are nearly 500 million Facebook users, making it the third largest country in the world. Facebook users were almost average in their level of interest in most areas when compared with users of Twitter, MySpace, and LinkedIn. Out of 45 categories, only national news, sports, exercise, travel, and home and garden skewed even slightly higher than average, and then by only one or two percentage points.

Ad Age magazine reports the Anderson study as stating that Facebookers are more likely to be married (40%), white (80%), and retired (6%) than users of other social networks. They have the second-highest average income, at $61,000, and an average of 121 connections. Facebook users skew a bit older and are more likely to be late adopters of social media. They are also extremely loyal to the site. 75% claim Facebook is their favorite site, and another 59% say they have increased their use of the site in the past six months.

c: Getting Fans for Your Facebook Fan Page

Using Facebook for brand promotion requires a Facebook fan page (aka Facebook business page). To obtain one, go to the bottom of your profile page, click on "advertising", and "go to pages". You will be given an incredibly long URL. To shorten your URL you are required to have a minimum of 25 fans.

Once you obtain those 25 or more fans, you can get your desired fan page vanity URL. This is much easier to remember and much shorter.

Now the fun begins, developing good and interesting content. You will find that most of your fans will **already** be your customers. Their loyalty is incredibly valuable and averages about $136 per fan:

Average Value of a Facebook Fan in North America, June 2010

Cost offset for fan acquisition $0.47

Earned media value $6.79

Recommendations $13.57

Loyalty $43.71

Spend $71.84

Note: total average value=$136.38 across the 20 brands included in the study
Source: Syncapse and Hotspex, "The Value of a Facebook Fan: An Empirical Review," provided to eMarketer, June 11, 2010

116457   www.eMarketer.com

A Facebook business/fan page helps you to communicate with consumers who are your most rabid fans and often your best revenue producers as the following chart of major corporations clearly shows:

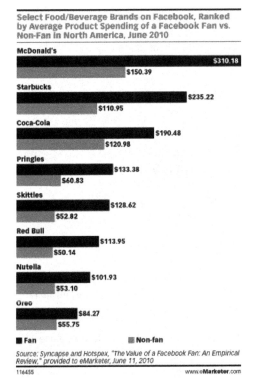

Select Food/Beverage Brands on Facebook, Ranked by Average Product Spending of a Facebook Fan vs. Non-Fan in North America, June 2010

McDonald's — $310.18 / $150.39
Starbucks — $235.22 / $110.95
Coca-Cola — $190.48 / $120.98
Pringles — $133.38 / $60.83
Skittles — $128.62 / $52.82
Red Bull — $113.95 / $50.14
Nutella — $101.93 / $53.10
Oreo — $84.27 / $55.75

■ Fan   ▓ Non-fan

Source: Syncapse and Hotspex, "The Value of a Facebook Fan: An Empirical Review," provided to eMarketer, June 11, 2010

116455   www.eMarketer.com

Here are some of the tips we have taken to heart to grow our fan page:

1. Develop an FBML **"Welcome"** tab at the top of your page that will be the first-time landing page and will contain a video explaining what you do and what you want the Facebook fan page to do for them. Ask them to click on the "like" button above and explain what's in it for them if they do.

2. Make sure that the **description box** underneath your logo contains a keyword-rich description of your organization and a "what's-in-it-for-you" for your fans, should they join.

3. Include a **link** to your Web site for more information.

4. Pull your **blog posts** into your Facebook fan page to give it fresh content and good SEO.

5. Add an **opt-in box** on your wall and offer your fans the opportunity to:

- Subscribe to your newsletter

- Download a free copy of your latest How-To video

- Obtain something free that they can only get by subscribing to your list such as a white paper, Webinar, coupons, discounts, etc.

You must provide a reason for your growing fan base to come back to your page again and again.

Here are a few tried and true ideas we use that can excite a fan base and help grow your following:

1. Create a **media calendar** for your posts and articles that you are pulling into your Facebook fan page. This will allow them to see what new content is coming up and when.

2. Offer your fans **exclusive deals** on your products and services that they can only get by being your fans.

3. Publish **short video messages** with good business tips and strategies that your fans can share with their friends.

4. Make sure your personal Facebook profile page clearly **lists the URL** of your fan page in the info tab AND in the bio section under your photo.

5. React to your fans with **direct messages**, as well as from your wall. Visit the profiles of your most engaged fans occasionally and acknowledge them. Comment on their page, their articles, or something they've done well recently. Show them that you really see them as valuable contributors to the page.

6. Don't be afraid to use **guest content providers** and guest video content on your fan page, and to promote others who have good content relevant to your services. It doesn't have to be all about you. Understand that "guest" contributing can be a little tricky. If you ask a "fan" to contribute content to your fan wall, that is easy. However, his or her contribution to your fan page will only be seen by those who actually visit the page. For those fans that rely on your content coming into their personal profile news feeds, this will NOT happen when the guest writes a comment. To make this work you need to assign the special guest contributor temporary "administrator" privileges. However, now when she/he posts on your fan page wall, your business icon will appear, NOT his/her picture, and you lose the feeling of a growing conversation.

Here is how we have overcome that problem:

1. Assign the guest "fan" temporary "admin" privileges. Now their posts will be seen by all fans on their own profile pages.

2. Add a head shot of the guest "fan" to your photo album on the site.

3. Have them pull up the photo and "share" it when they write their post.

4. Have them sign their post with their name.

5. If they want to have another picture alongside their own head shot, they can have that or alternatively, a video or link.

6. Now you have overcome one of Facebook fan page's major obstacles, in our consideration, and that is a lack of conversation going on in the page that can be multiplied by "fans" and their friends being able to see it on their profile pages. This is a quantum step in the right direction.

Once you are in the habit of providing a useful Facebook fan page environment, you can extend your outreach beyond Facebook:

1. Make sure you shout-out about new blog articles, videos, or other content pulled into your fan page on Twitter, LinkedIn, and other social media.

2. Include your Facebook fan page link in your blog articles.

3. Add your Facebook fan page link to your signature on all of your e-mails.

4. List your Facebook fan page address on your business cards.

5. Develop an e-newsletter that expands the information on your fan page and tell them about new content, events, etc., coming to your fan page.

6. Develop your key influencer list and spend time every week befriending people who are influencers and who have large followings in the communities you want to reach. This is done in your profile page and on other platforms, such as LinkedIn. Once you find them, gently invite them to your fan page.

7. Growing your Twitter broadcasting reach can substantially affect your Facebook fan page numbers. Especially if (after a while) you invite tweeters to join the conversation on your facebook fan page.

Once you have notified all your "friends" about your new fan page, your email list, Twitter followers and exhausted every other avenue of contact then it is time to get serious. NOTHING will grow your "fans" on facebook faster than a good offer and a Google AdWords advertising campaign. For a few dollars every month you will provide continual growth for the Facebook fan page.

Your fans are valuable because they are far more likely to buy your product or service repeatedly over many years. They are more brand-loyal as the chart from eMarketer.com below shows:

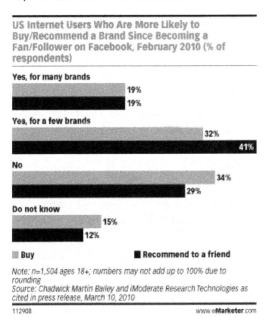

US Internet Users Who Are More Likely to Buy/Recommend a Brand Since Becoming a Fan/Follower on Facebook, February 2010 (% of respondents)

Yes, for many brands
- 19%
- 19%

Yes, for a few brands
- 32%
- 41%

No
- 34%
- 29%

Do not know
- 15%
- 12%

▨ Buy   ■ Recommend to a friend

Note: n=1,504 ages 18+; numbers may not add up to 100% due to rounding
Source: Chadwick Martin Bailey and iModerate Research Technologies as cited in press release, March 10, 2010

112908   www.eMarketer.com

d) The Formula for Success on Facebook

This next section is from Social Media Examiner, written by social media consultant **Amy Porterfield**, http://amyporterfield.com, http://www.socialmediaexaminer.com/4-proven-steps-to-facebook-page-success/#more-3907, 2009, and is one of the best articles on the growth of Facebook fan pages that I have read. In this article, Amy offers the idea that a strategy behind a Facebook page does not need to be complicated.

You can apply Amy's simple formula in four steps:

> **Vision + Branding + Inbound Marketing + Engagement = A Rock-Solid Facebook Page**

#1: Create a Compelling Vision

To back up her formula, Amy Porterfield gives an excellent example of a case study from the California State Parks Foundation:

In an attempt to save 210 state parks from closing, the foundation hired Adams Hussey & Associates to help create the "Friend Get a Friend" campaign. The campaign was created to **promote awareness and discussion** around the looming park closures and to encourage people to take action to save their local state parks.

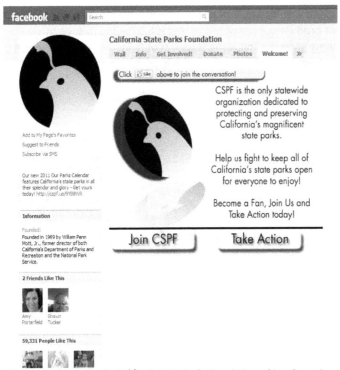

This Facebook page for the California State Parks Foundation achieved amazing media exposure.

As Amy suggests, the California State Parks Foundation has a noble cause, much like a favorite charity or saving the planet, but what about just a simple product or service without much planet saving capability?

Dairy Queen is an example of one such organization that provides an excellent product but possibly one that is NOT going to save the World. Amy gives the following screen shot from Dairy Queen, which has an extremely successful page with loyal followers:

The Dairy Queen page has nearly two million fans

Amy says of Dairy Queen: "Their mission is not necessarily going to change the world—but **the people behind the brand are passionate and committed to creating an experience and making their customers happy**—and that kind of passion is contagious. (Take note—you can **create the same kind of excitement for your brand as well!**)"

#2: Smart Branding

Amy points out that some of the most successful pages look like mini-websites inside of Facebook. With the advent of FBML (Facebook markup language), it is possible to dress up your Facebook landing page to follow the branding guidelines of your Web site and other key promotional materials.

However, a word of caution: Facebook is still in the realm of social media. You are having a "conversation" with your consumers or fans. Don't make it too sales- or promotion-oriented. Make it a source of information on your thought leadership subject, or a place where they can get information or deals that they can't get anywhere else including your Web site. Leave your Web site as the mother ship for promoting what you do and keep the Facebook fan page as a great information source. Always remember to push from Facebook to your Web site.

Will a Facebook fan page replace a brand's Web site someday? In some instances, quite possibly. For major brands or organizations where the product or services needs extensive explanation, Facebook will supplement the brand's Web site not replace it. The value of having a branded Facebook page is obviously a great draw.

Amy states, "Branding is key to making your page serve as a mini-hub for all your customers and prospects that are likely spending a lot of their time on the social networking site already." To understand this, Amy offers another great example of a company that has mastered the concept of the "mini-hub" inside Facebook. Chick-fil-A, a popular fast-food chain in the U.S., has a thriving page with over 1.5 million fans.

Not only do they offer coupons regularly, they also display their menu and their "coming soon" specials inside their page.

#3: Strategic Inbound Marketing

Amy suggests that many Facebook fan page owners don't apply the same inbound marketing strategies they use for their Web sites. The use of search engine optimization and cross promotion from **all** Internet marketing sources is vital.

Amy worked with the founder of Social Media Examiner, Mike Stelzner, to create their Facebook Social Media Examiner page, which already has over 8,000 fans.

It is an excellent example of cross promotion. Utilizing their email blasts to more than 26,000 readers, they encouraged them to join the Social Media Examiner fan page. It added about a 100 new fans daily.

#4: Real-Time Engagement

Lastly, Amy reminds us that Facebook is a **social** platform, and without engagement, it becomes a static Web page. As Amy states, "the rule for engagement is to **make it about your fans and not about you.** (Remember that people love to talk about themselves—so craft your articles and questions around them, and you're sure to see some great conversations begin to surface on your page.)"

e: The Art of Tweet

According to a group of researchers at Korea's Advanced Institute of Science and Technology http://www.kisti.re.kr/english/, Twitter is not a very social network. After analyzing over 41 million user profiles and 1.47 billion follower/following relationships, the researchers concluded that only 22% of all connections on Twitter are reciprocal. On Flickr, this number is closer to 68% and on Yahoo 360 it's 84%. The large majority (78%) of connections between users on Twitter are one-way relationships. (Reported by Frederic Lardinois , May 11, 2010, http://www.readwriteweb.com/archives/study_twitter_isnt_very_soc ial.php)

More notable is that 68% of all Twitter users aren't followed by a single person they are following. As the researchers rightly note, this makes Twitter more like a broadcast medium than a social network.

Given that Twitter was set up for these kinds of non-reciprocal follower/following relationships, it doesn't come as a surprise that many users would use Twitter to follow breaking news channels and celebrities. The fact that almost 80% of these relationships are one-way hints that Twitter's mainstream users use the service more as a **news medium** than as a social network.

Any viewing of a Twitter page will show that a good 65% of Tweets contain a **URL** at the end. This means that Twitter is being used to show people the path to more information, more content, someone's blog or Web site or white paper.

Here is the secret to growing your Twitter followers in an organized manner, populated with people who meet your target profile: **Follow the people you want to follow you!** The unwritten (not always observed law of Twitter) is that if you follow me, I will follow you. At least till I find you don't provide good content.

The best way to find people who meet your target profile is to find them in a hash tag group. Hash tag groups are people with a common interest who have agreed to follow each other using the collector code of # (a hash tag).

One of the ways of finding groups that meet your profile requirements is to go to hashtags.org and type a word that seems to fit your requirements for the profile. In my case, it would be "social media". The chart at the top of the Web page will show you the volume of use for that particular hash tag. Run your mouse over the user names listed below them to see which hash tag they belong to.

Once you have isolated one or two hash tags to follow then go to www.blastfollow.com or a similar program:

Plug in your hash tag group's name, hit "Get Users", and within minutes, you will be following everyone in that group. Be prepared however to either have an auto responder like Tweepi direct response everyone who has decided to follow you back, (which will be the majority). I personally prefer a personally written direct response but I also have a message scheduled to go out two days after I am informed that someone is following me.

The following section on using Twitter more as a promotional media is adapted from an article by Cindy King at http://www.socialmediaexaminer.com, published May 12, 2010:

1: Twitter Events: Cindy informs us that these allow people to network at specific times with larger groups of people by the use of hash tags. Twitter events can help you find people to build your own Twitter network. As you participate in these events, you will increase your Twitter authority on the topics you discuss. You can even create your own Twitter events to drive your networking and social media marketing.

2: Types of Twitter Events: Cindy states that in step number one, you need to **identify the groups of people with whom you wish to network**. Then you should choose the types of events where it's easy and comfortable for you to network with these people. This is how you can slowly build up meaningful one-on-one relationships with people who matter to you and to your business. Fortunately, there are several different types of groups gathering around specific topics on Twitter at specific times.

Here are events that take place **offline** where people use Twitter as a communication tool to share their experience of the in-person event:

3: Live events: You have probably seen Twitter hash tags used by people tweeting from conferences. People can tweet about any kind of live event. If you want to get the most out of your Twitter networking at a live event, you should do as Adam Vincenzini says and plan ahead to ensure viral Twitter coverage of live events.

4:Twestivals: These get people using Twitter to meet up all over the world.

5: Current events: Many businesses can benefit from staying current on trending topics and participating in relevant Twitter conversations. Some current events or breaking news may give you reason to create your own Twitter discussion or chat event.

6: Twitter Interviews: You can conduct Twitter interviews (http://www.socialmediaexaminer.com/7-steps-to-successful-twitter-interviews/) with different communication goals. You can do the interview like a journalist or, as this is on Twitter, you can conduct it more like a game show, with a short set of questions aimed at having more fun. Choose the kind of Twitter interview to use to give you the networking environment you prefer.

7: TweetChats: There are a number of regularly scheduled TweetChats. Small Business Buzz (http://sbbuzz.wordpress.com/), or @sbbuzz (http://twitter.com/sbbuzz) on Twitter, holds chats every Tuesday to discuss small business topics. Another interesting regular TweetChat takes place on Thursdays, @lrnchat (http://twitter.com/lrnchat) to discuss learning and social media (http://lrnchat.wordpress.com/). It's easy to see how you can expand your Twitter network by finding TweetChats with your preferred audience.

8: Host a Tweetup: A Tweetup is a live event promoted virtually through Twitter. Depending on your number of followers and re-tweets, it can be a great addition. However, don't use it exclusively if you are looking for large numbers; also use ads, e-mail, direct mail, etc.

9: Tools for Twitter Events: Many Twitter applications come and go, but they often have some great features and make Twitter networking easier and more fun. Unfortunately, there isn't a solution to fit all of your needs in following or creating Twitter events, so it's always worthwhile doing a little research to look for what's useful for you.

Here are some Twitter applications you may find interesting:

TweetChat (http://tweetchat.com/), Tweetvite (http://tweetvite.com/), and TweetMyEvents (http://tweetmyevents.com/).

a) **Hash tags:** As mentioned before, hash tags are of key importance. They enable people to gather into groups on Twitter. This is how you find others interested in similar topics.

b) **Event tools:** Sometimes you simply need an event management tool. There are a variety of online tools to help you: Eventbrite (http://www.eventbrite.com/), Amiando (http://www.amiando.com/), and Meetup (http://www.meetup.com/) are popular event tools. Again, you will need to check them out to find the one best suited to your particular needs.

c) **Blastfollow:** The unspoken rule in Twitter land is that if I follow you, and I provide good content, you will follow me. You can't follow me if you don't know I exist. The key tool in completing the task of finding each other is to locate the # (hash tag) groups in which you are interested. The groups I belong to are #socialmedia, #tourismchat, and #sm. Plug those into Blastfollow.com and you will be following those people in a matter of hours. Many of them will follow you back. Keeping them may be another matter.

f) LinkedIn - The Business Blog

LinkedIn users:
It is probably no surprise that these "guys" are all about business. Ad Age says "guys" because LinkedIn has the only user group with more males than females (57% to 43%). They have the highest average income, at $89,000. They are more likely to have joined the site for business or work, citing keeping in touch with business friends, job searching, business development, and recruiting as top reasons for joining.

Their interests reflect that as well. They like all kinds of news, employment information, sports, and politics. They are also more likely to be into the gym, spas, yoga, golf, and tennis.

Excluding video-game systems, they own more electronic gadgets than those from any other social networks. These gadgets include digital cameras, high-definition TVs, DVRs, and Blu-ray players.

How do they unwind? Strangely, they are more interested in gambling and soap operas than other social media users. Some 12% seek gambling information online (versus an average of 7%); while 10% go online for soap opera content (versus an average of 5%).

g) YouTube and Video Sharing

For the sake of this discussion, I am going to use the name "YouTube" to describe all of the video sharing sites on the Web.

Other microblog and social platforms can be used to make announcements, point the way, regurgitate news, and have people get to know you in a non-threatening manner.

So where does YouTube fit in? YouTube is the flesh behind the tweet, the face behind the blog.

It could be said that your video content puts meat on your skeletal bones. There is another answer to this question: Some people are visual and auditory, while others like to read. Here is what YouTubers tend to look like:

YouTube Demographics:

<18	**18%**
18-34	**20%**
35-44	**19%**
45-54	**21%**
55+	**21%**

For under $200 (at time of this writing), you can get yourself a reasonably good quality Flip video camera. Small and simple to use and even easier to edit, they can be carried in your pocket. I have an expensive HD Cannon video camera and editing suite that I use for big projects, but I love my little Flip.

Now you understand that video helps flesh out your personality and your brand. It gives a face, voice and humanity to your blog, your microblogs and your Web site. If you include it on your Web site, it is also great for search engine rankings.

But, what are you going to video about? One of the videos can be a short expansion of your blog content, so that it is educational and of value to the viewer. You can pull this into your Web site or Facebook Welcome page. I use video to sell my **HPR** Public relations and Social Media business, my books, seminars, and public speaking events. These I tend to send privately via email or put on YouTube as a "not for public" viewing video, and then embed it into my Web site or blog, but that's just me.

I do take video snippets of my seminars and speeches and place them on my Web site so that meeting planners can see that I am not a complete idiot.

I also use video to explain my seminars in a fun, short manner and allow the meeting planners to email them out either to attendees of the conference to promote my session, or to potential attendees to the conference to promote attendance. These are powerful promotional tools for conference attendance.

One of my YouTube gurus is Perry Belcher (http://www.perrybelcher.com/). Perry gets his point across in a simple and easy manner. Here I have paraphrased his "10 Top YouTube Tips" that I use, and they work:

1. Perry says that you don't have to be fancy or have expensive editing software. In fact, it is less trusted than the glitzy Hollywood production.

2. Perry likes to talk directly into the camera and keep it simple.

3. He says to make sure you tell them who you are and how they can get hold of you.

4. Only cover 3-6 points on the video and remember--YouTube will cut you off at 15 minutes. Keep it under 3 minutes for max attention.

5. Ask for comments and embeds.

6. If you are using a white board to present, make sure that your name, URL, Twitter account, and any other addresses you want them to follow is on the top line of the white board.

7. He reminds us to thank them for watching; it's simply good manners.

8.   Use a screen shot of your video and put it in your emails.

Embed your video into your blog, Web site or Facebook fan page.

When you Tweet about the release of your video and you use a tiny URL put the URL destination beside it, like this: http://tiny.cc/9hiUQ (my Web site) this will increase clicks.

There is a lot more to learn, but that will get you started. Remember all of your social networking is a little like a blind Internet date: It doesn't get real until they get to see your face and hear your voice...and that's on YouTube.

As social media-minded executives are well aware, video blogs (vlogs) have experienced massive growth over the last several years—and it appears a handful of video hosting sites are now dominating the field, according to newly released figures from Heredia, a video search engine tracking more than 30,000 sources across the Web. Here's how the major players rank:

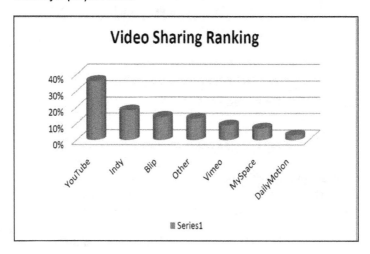

h) Podcasts:

One of the social media platforms given the least attention these days are podcasts. Podcasts are an audio or video program (yes, the concept of iCarly.com could be considered a podcast), formatted to be played back on iPods, other MP3 players, or off a Web site and made available for free or for purchase over the Internet.

Podcasts are shows, similar to radio or TV shows produced by professionals or amateurs and posted to the Internet for downloading, listening to, or viewing. Many podcasts are made available free of charge, though some ask to be purchased.

Podcasts can be downloaded individually or subscribed to so that each new episode of the podcast is automatically downloaded to the subscriber's computer. You can subscribe to a podcast at the iTunes Store or Web sites for the podcasts. Podcast subscriptions are usually facilitated using RSS feeds.

Podcasts are one more way you can promote your brand message. They are especially effective when placed on your Website, like the podcast news archive on Cisco's Web site: (http://tools.cisco.com/newsroom/contactSearch/archive/?type=pod) as it then expands your knowledge leadership and perceived expertise.

Podcasts' advantage over a vlog is the time and expense that it takes to produce the content, and the ease with which it can be transported by its consumers (on iPods and MP3s) once downloaded.

Because of its ease to produce and distribute, many podcast channels have been established. I broadcast my podcasts on, http://socialmedialeaders.podbean.com/, where I interview top people in their field regarding social media strategy.

I am a great fan of http://www.commoncraft.com/, which produces simple videos on many subjects. One of their best is on understanding podcasting in plain English.

Fitting podcasts into your social media strategy for brand promotion is an important consideration. We call Facebook, MySpace, LinkedIn, Twitter, etc., microblogs because of their limited writing wall space and the fact that they are used often to point people to additional sources of information through tiny URLs. However, a vlog and a podcast can also act as a macroblog if you remember to point them in the direction of your Web site.

All of the aforementioned social media platforms are wonderful but without **"engagement"** there is no social in social media. It is like a megaphone without a voice, or a cell phone without someone to call; they are inanimate technologies.

Secret Three:

The Power of Social Media is "Engagement"

It is very easy to have "follower" envy in social media. When I see people who have 14,000 followers on Twitter or 2,000 fans on Facebook I writhe with envy. However it is far more appropriate to have "engagement" envy, (I don't mean the kind that leads to marriage).

The people I really envy are people who have developed a following through **engagement**. This is the most difficult and least understood part of social media. It is as tricky to continually get meaningful engagement virtually as it is in real life!

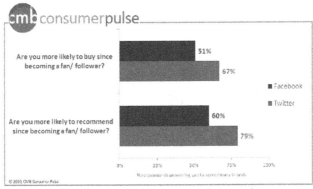

Chadwick Martin Bailey http://blog.cmbinfo.com/smreport/

a: It's All About Buzz

The more I think about it the more I begin to realize that Richard
Florida is right in his book *"The Rise of the Creative Class"* (2002).
http://www.amazon.com/Rise-Creative-Class-Transforming-
Community/dp/0465024769):

> **Nearly every creative person becomes a brand unto themselves.**
> **Every definition of "brand management" is as relevant to creative**
> **individuals, just as much as a running shoe or a package of cereal.**

Let's say you have identified your communities and set up your
Community Managers and you have a bunch of busy bees that
understand every nuance of the Twitter, Facebook, LinkedIn, or
YouTube platforms, and are just itching to slave away on your behalf.
A couple of months down the road you get a rather nagging feeling
that nothing much is happening. Oh yes, they are blogging, yes they
are tweeting, and yes there are podcasts and vlogs galore, but
whatever metrics you have set up for your success just aren't budging.

Well, first, if you are like me, you most likely really haven't given much
thought about units of measurement for success or failure in the social
networking arena. Is it going to be the number of blog views? Is it the
number of followers on Twitter, friends or fans on Facebook, eyeballs
on YouTube or great consumer comments on FourSquare or Yelp?

The answer is most likely all of the above but the bottom line is
that one of the leading metrics for social media is Return On
Engagement (ROE), and that ROE is measured in conversations, NOT
conversions. These conversations we simply call "buzz." If you can't
generate buzz it becomes very difficult to accomplish the higher-level
metrics such as unique users added to the brand's Web site.

If your Managers are not creating buzz in their respective communities, then nothing is really happening and time is not being productively.

> **Author Mark Hughes defines buzz as "capturing the attention of consumers and the media to the point where talking about your brand or destination becomes entertaining, fascinating and newsworthy."** (*Buzzmarketing: Get People to Talk About Your Stuff*, 2008. http://www.buzzmarketing.com/about.html)

Real buzz continues for three or more conversations in depth. This can be a re-tweet, or a wall conversation on Facebook that takes off, but it needs to be picked up and carried a minimum of three times or more to start to be considered buzz.

What you have done is started people gossiping about you around the virtual water cooler. Gossip is a good word to describe buzz because people want to find out if the gossip is true or not and so will carry the conversation further.

Will this buzz happen every day? No. Should it happen a couple of times a month? Yes, that would be nice. Buzz is the home run of social networking.

One of the dangers of buzz (or gossip) is that your message will go way off track. It is a bit like that silly exercise we used to do in school where you start whispering something to see how it ends up after 20 or more people have whispered it to each other.

Keeping control of the message is, in my view, part of the role of legacy media, including print advertising, TV, and radio. Social media sows the ground and makes it fertile for the legacy-advertising message.

What Creates Buzz?

Mark Hughes has noted six things that tend to push people's buttons and create buzz more than all others. I have taken the liberty (sorry Mark) of adding a seventh. Here they are:

1. The taboo (sex, lies, bathroom humor)

2. The unusual

3. The outrageous

4. The hilarious

5. The remarkable

6. Secrets revealed

7. Top 10 lists (my feeble addition)

Now, don't look at that list and say, "My boss would never let me write that!" Everything can be adapted. Remember the more you white wash, the less effective it will become. No one wants you to become a sensationalist, but a little naughty can be fun. It's up to you.

Here are some examples used in Mark's book *Buzz Marketing*. In the slightly taboo category, do you remember Proctor & Gamble's "Don't Squeeze the Charmin"? Of course you do, everyone does. Mr. Whipple would admonish people in the store to resist squeezing the Charmin. He tapped into our taboo and what did we do when we saw Charmin in the grocery store? Right, we squeezed. It was the most successful campaign in P&G's history.

In the "unusual" category, Ian Klein went into the online dating business in 2000, and competed against giants such as Match.com. His sister was one of 64% of overweight Americans who were single at the time, so he created OverweightDate.com.

Soon the gossip started at Weight Watchers, singles bars, everywhere where people were struggling with their weight. Best of all, his idea worked!

I only use these examples from Mark Hughes' book because they show you that you don't have to be over the top to tap into the gossip gene pool.

So, now, you have used the above and created some buzz. However, what kind of buzz is picked up and run with in legacy media the most? In other words, which buzz become stories that have legs?

Here are the five most frequently written stories year after year:

1.   The David and Goliath story

2.   The unusual story

3.   The controversy story

4.   The celebrity story

5.   What's hot in the media

You want examples? Of course, you do. Well the media is littered with David and Goliath stories, small companies going up against Fortune 500 companies, getting bloodied but winning (or at least going the 10 rounds). It's the Rocky story over and over again. Everyone loves it. Think Delorian going up against Detroit. It didn't end well but that wasn't because of Detroit (or was it...) How about Ben and Jerry's versus Haagen-Dazs? The stories repeat. You get the picture.

Another guru of mine is Mari Smith (http://www.marismith.com/), not just because she hails from Scotland (and so do I), or that she is now Canadian (so was I), but because she is my guru of Facebook. I quote from her:

> **"Today, it is not just who you know, but who knows YOU."**
> **Mari Smith, www.marismith.com**

Monitoring Your Buzz

I reviewed an excellent article in the *Wall Street Journal* by Sarah Needleman (http://muckrack.com/sarahneedleman) a short while ago. It was about the growing number of businesses tracking social media comments on platforms such as Facebook and Twitter. In the article, Sarah reported how these major companies are tracking social media to gauge consumer sentiment, and avert potential public relations disasters.

Although I prefer to concentrate on the positive, business-building side of social networking for **HPR** clients, social media does provide a resource that has not been available in the past to monitor the mood of the marketplace and provide an avenue for good Public relations, if done in a timely fashion.

According to Sarah, Ford Motor Company, PepsiCo Inc., and Southwest Airlines, among many others, all deploy software and assign employees to monitor Internet articles and blogs. They're also assigning senior leaders to craft corporate strategies for social media.

At Ford, Sarah explains, Twitter messages alerted Ford's head of social media to comments "criticizing Ford for allegedly trying to shut a fan Web site, TheRangerStation.com. The dispute prompted about 1,000 email complaints to Ford overnight."

Sarah reported that Ford acted quickly, posting messages on Twitter pages assuring people that they were looking into the matter.

Ford added frequent updates as they learned more. "Within hours, Ford's lawyers withdrew the shut-down request, as long as the site would halt sales. By the end of the day, Ford tweeted that the dispute had been resolved."

Ford's quick response retained the founder of TheRangerStation.com as a customer, and earned it praise from social media experts.

Sarah also noted that critical Twitter posts caused PepsiCo to intensify its media efforts when "an ad in a German trade magazine for a diet cola, which depicted a calorie killing itself. A popular commentator, whose sister had committed suicide, asked, 'How could Pepsi do this?'

Apologies were quickly published on the personal Twitter pages of a Pepsi spokesperson, and of Pepsi's global director of digital and social media. This incident led to Pepsi's creation of a corporate Twitter Profile, and its participation on the networking site BlogHer.com.

Sarah also stated in her article that information shared on social media platforms also helped companies shape their policy in response to news. For example, following the emergency landing of one of its flights, Southwest Airlines searched social media sites for the reactions of passengers onboard. The comments were mostly positive, and the social media team at Southwest reacted accordingly, re-posting the praising statements.

If the passengers had been more critical, it would have elicited a different response from the Southwest Airlines team. "We would still be complimentary of our crews, but we might not have emphasized the passenger comments as much," reported Southwest's vice president, communications and strategic outreach.

Once a particular problem is spotted, then follow your public relations guidelines. If you haven't created any, do so quickly.

Make sure the following points are included in those PR guidelines:

1. Acknowledge the problem rapidly and inform the writer that you will look into it (not fix it, unless you can).

2. Don't be corporate or defensive.

3. Give them a timeline about when you will get back to them. This doesn't mean you have had to fix the problem by then, just that you will update them.

4. Keep to that timeline at all costs or you will make the problem worse.

5. Once the problem is (hopefully) resolved, follow up with them once or twice to keep in touch.

6. Thank them for helping the organization get better.

7. If you can't fix the problem, be honest and within the realm of legal obligations, be up front about why the problem can't be fixed.

8. If a third party has created the problem, let the third party know about the problem and get a response about fixing it. However, YOU remain as the contact for the person that has the problem, and have the third party respond through you. Do NOT obfuscate your responsibility.

b) How to Make Your Social Media Heard

Integrating social media into your marketing plan so it synergistically supports the whole effort is paramount to success. Although social media can support sales, as stated earlier, it really fits best (but not exclusively) under **Public Relations**.

This section concentrates on the art of developing public relations "hooks" in your content, whether it is for a blog, tweet or press releases.

If social media falls under **Public Relations**, then how many "publics" are in PR? Well the "public" is plural and does not refer to just one "public" but to at least seven:

1. Media relations

2. Employee relations

3. Community relations

4. Educator relations

5. Consumer relations

6. Stakeholder relations

7. Management relations

Media Relations:

The rise of the Internet and in particular the rise of "search" has affected all seven publics but perhaps none more than **media relations**. (It is strange that a new media has affected an old media.) This is happening while traditional media is in serious decline.

Today there are more people getting their news from Internet sources and bloggers than from newspapers or TV, as SEO-PR guru Greg Jarboe (http://www.seo-pr.com/public-relations-firms-boston-and-san-francisco.shtml) demonstrated at a PRWeb Webinar in November (http://www.seo-pr.com)

As Jarboe explained, daily newspaper circulation is dropping nationwide! A Web media release posted online with the Huffington Post generates three times more Web site visits than the same report on ABC News.

What are you looking for? a) Interested eyeballs that actually "open" and "read" your press releases or; b) the vague possibility of an "impression"? Are you trying to attract a consumer who is only interested in the general theme of a certain magazine or TV show but not necessarily your story?

Very few magazines have staff writers any more, and the freelance stringers will very rarely interview you in person. In fact, some will pose questions and ask for answers over Twitter.

However, obtaining media attention has not changed. What has changed in Public relations is the platform of delivery. In using Internet press releases, you still need to influence and engage the media's interest and this requires the use of "hooks".

Hooks:
Following is a reference from an excellent article about hooks by Pam Lontos (http://PrPr.net/hook-the-media/). It is explains how you can differentiate yourself from your competitors in troubled economic times:

Pam suggests in her article that the best way to attract more clients and customers is to create a level of celebrity for yourself that only the media can bring, and because today's media are more fragmented than ever before, you will need to reach out to many different types.

Pam says that while they all do things a bit differently and cover different topics, one thing will remain consistent when it comes to you getting coverage—the ability to develop a great hook.

Even though one publication may appeal to a narrow audience, an Internet news site may focus on a single topic, or a radio talk show may address just one subject line, you can still appeal to them all-if you have a great hook.

> **What is a hook? According to Pam, it is the essence of your story, the angle, the concept that can be boiled down to a few words. In a way, your hook is the bait, like a headline that makes someone want to read the whole story.**

I have used hooks for many key promotions over the years. Let's face it: most products are basically boring, except to their owners. The hook makes it interesting by relating to a secondary event that is far more interesting and valuable to the reader. Sometimes I feel I should buy a stamp that says "boring" and bang it down on silly, boring products. It's the hook that makes them sizzle.

The product when presented to the media, either over the Internet or by an old-time press release, needs to be presented with the angle of a hook.

As an example, back in the day (don't ask), I had to promote the opening of a beautiful nightclub called "Darlings", at a Four Seasons Hotel. Now, you would think that just letting the press know a new nightclub was opening, especially at a Four Seasons Hotel, would bring them out in droves. Well, possibly, but the article would come out after the event and the opening is what creates the buzz. In addition, there were two other clubs opening almost at the same time, hence diluting our story. What would our hook be?

Our hook was a pre-opening promotion playing on the name of the club...Darlings, that generated a lot of "buzz" and press all by itself.

Three months prior to opening, we created two mailing lists. The first list consisted of upwardly mobile young men, the second, of upwardly mobile young women.

After creating the two lists we mailed what looked like handwritten little notes (they were actually printed) to the people on each list, saying, "I miss you Darling" on the first, "I want you Darling" on the next, and finally "Meet me Darling" on the last note. The final mailing was a beautiful invitation that said, "Meet Me Tuesday Night for the opening of 'Darlings'."

We did not have to generate press; the public flooded the post office to find out who was mailing these notes. Jilted lovers threatened to sue if they found out. Headlines read, "Public Wants to Know Who is Sending Love Notes?"

There were 2,700 people lined up to get into the Darlings nightclub on opening night to a club could hold only 500. It was the "hook" that created the buzz, not the nightclub. However, what kept them coming back time and again was the quality of the nightclub experience.

c: Engaging through Search:

SEO is still one of the most vital components of your Internet marketing strategy (including social media).

It would be impossible to write a book that can keep up with the changing Google algorithms but here are some key ideas you can use to keep your content available for SEO:

Step 1: Develop an editorial calendar. This will MAKE you think about what articles you are going to research and write about.

You can look at your editorial calendar through a "seasonal" lens i.e., winter, spring, summer, etc. Alternatively, by sales season, or which products are selling at what time. You can ask your industry magazines for their editorial calendars, check to see what they are writing about, and follow suit. Here is an example of our last editorial calendar:

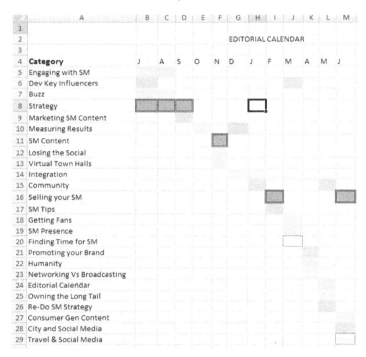

Step 2: Make a list of the trunk key words, long tail key words, and phrases that naturally go with each blog article, tweet or Facebook posting.

Step 3: Test the key words on http://freekeywords.wordtracker.com/ or Web CEO or other platforms that assist in giving you a sense of how many people search using those key words.

FREE keyword suggestion tool

Keyword	Searches (?)
Social Media 3,167 searches (top 100 only)	Want more *Social Media* keywords?
1 social media (search)	724
2 social media marketing (search)	525
3 social media news release (search)	220
4 articles about using social media as a marketing tool (search)	78
5 social media optimization (search)	75
6 social media icons (search)	72
7 what is social media (search)	72
8 small business social media (search)	70
9 social media press release (search)	58
10 social media sites (search)	44
11 social media savannah (search)	42
12 public scrutiny of the work of social workers through the media doesnt effect their service delivery (search)	32

There are two kinds of search terms. First there are "trunk" key words. These are the obvious words such as in the case of my business, "social media".

Secondly, there are "long tail" key words or phrases that are less used but also have less competition from other search engines. Confused, read on!

Using trunk key words such as "social media", shown in the slide above, will gain you the most number of searches. However, trunk key words may NOT be the most expedient way to gain followers or visits to your Web site or Facebook fan page, because the competition is very high and you will most likely end up on page 3 or 4 of the search results page (SRP).

The Power of Long Tail Key Words:

The power of long tail keywords is best explained by the Key Effectiveness Indicator (KEI). Web CEO, (a free download, http://www.webceo.com/), has coined the phrase "Key Effectiveness Indicator". A Key Effectiveness Indicator (KEI) is a mathematical formula of the relationship between the number of Web sites that respond to a search term and the actual number of searches over a given period of time.

The KEI is demonstrated in the slide below. The search phrase "social media" elicits 273 million responses. Monthly searches are approximately 229,300. This produces a KEI score of .214. A better score would be .014 which is "social media monitoring" on line five, giving a KEI of .014. This means that although the number of monthly searches is lower (9,100), I have a better chance of ranking high on the SRP because there are only 6 million competitors rather than 273 million.

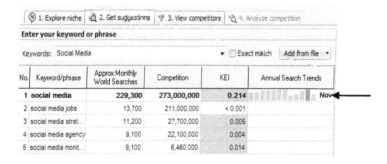

An interesting feature of Web CEO is the **Annual Search Trends** (arrow above). This bar graph shows when the key search phrase is MOST used during the year. This is a powerful tool for online marketing. Beginning a Pay Per Click campaign the month before (in this case October) and carry it through the key month (November) will add powerfully to your results.

In my business, the keyword people use to search would be "social media," but look what happens when I search that term:

197 million blogs and Web sites appear. EEK! It means I am battling 197 million people for page one of the search results page. This is why, you see on the right side of the slide, I run a little Google advertisement for my blog, www.buzzmaster.wordpress.com.

However, if I use a less-used "long tail" keyword, such as "How to promote your brand on social media," then I am only battling 32 million and my blog actually pops up on page one:

d) Engaging Through Key Influencers

Why bother with all the continued work regarding "key influencers?" A mention about my blog from a key influencer, say David Meerman Scott (http://www.webinknow.com/) in his blog about social media, is huge. It is important not only in the number of his readers that will click to my blog and read it, but, if the content is sticky enough, they will hopefully come back repeatedly.

Another example would be a Twitter mention from travel marketing guru Bill Geist (http://www.billgeist.typepad.com/), or in his blog or e-newsletter. These all create credibility within the community you are trying to reach.

Here are eight ways I find my key influencers in the community I write about, that of social media:

1. http://technorati.com/entertainment/glosslip/

2. http://search.twitter.com/advanced

3. http://del.icio.us/tag/topic+blog

4. http://www.google.com/alerts

5. http://stumbleupon.com

6. http://aiderss.com

7. Hashtags in Twitter

8. http://www.big-boards.com/

Another key source often overlooked is your local bookstore. Many of the top people in any community also publish. So, whether it is birding, skiing, carousel making, hot air ballooning, or whatever the community is, you may find the top key influencers are published.

Also, check Amazon.com or Lulu.com because there may be self-published books from authors with a key influence.

What are other values of key influencers? First, of course, they multiply your reach. Secondly they can sometimes be persuaded to become guest contributors to your social media content which gives you great credibility. Don't forget, in the social media as Marie Smith says, it is not just who you know but who knows you.

Another value is just the fact they know who you are in the industry. It can be very damning to a potential client to hear the comment "nope, never heard of him".

Let me give you an example: Some wonderful folks from Canada contacted my office last year to see if I could speak at their conference. It happened to fit perfectly into a time slot that I was planning to be in Canada (although not exactly that part of Canada, it is *so* big) and so we said we would love to be considered.

One of the questions we always ask our leads, "how did you find us?" Well here is the five-step path they took, as far as I can figure it:

1. They contacted the office of one of my key influencers, Bill Geist, and spoke to Terri (Bill's High Priestess of Client Services), who suggested me (thank you, Terri!).

2. Then they searched and went to my Web site, www.johnhopejohnstone.com.

3. From there they read one of the posts on my Buzz Master blog.

4. Then read my professional profile on LinkedIn.

5. Then I emailed a Flip video (I could have put it on YouTube).

See how each of these steps is a step down a path to find out more about you and your organization?

These paths can follow many different routes back and forth between the social platforms, but the results are the same. People get to know you a little better each time they visit a social media platform.

In this instance, they used a **personal reference** (Terri) who knew of my book, and then expanded by going to my **Web site**. They then could have deepened it by going to **my blog**, followed me on **Twitter** (@HopeJohnstone), and saw me in the flesh through a Flip video snippets of a past seminar, emailed from **You Tube**.

Other folks have followed me on Twitter, then read my blog for a while, then read a bit more about me on my Web site, perhaps read one of my books, then met someone who knows me or has heard me speak...Well, you get the picture.

e) 20 Rules of Engagement:

We are going to suppose that you have created your "key influencer list" and that now you are ready to pull them into your sphere of influence. Some of the people on your list you may already know (these are the low hanging fruit). Others you will have heard of but may not have met eyeball-to-eyeball (high fructose).

Ok, so pick up the phone, call them, and say...what? Most likely not even get hold of them; just leave some rambling message like an idiot.

You could send them an email (which is still valid). If you do decide to use the email route then make sure you have a mutual friend in common: "Hi, Harry! Gloria suggested that I send you an email as we are mutual friends." The problem now is that you really have to go into your pitch RIGHT NOW! Such as "Harry, would you go to my Web site and see if you like my product? Click here." Hmm, a bit pushy even if you do have Gloria in common, but it might work.

Here are 20 tips to improving your engagement strategy:

1. Remember. Your key influencer list is gold. It is the quality not quantity that counts.

2. Have an engagement strategy. Why are you doing all this work? Where are you going?

3. Always send a personal note (online) when you ask to become a LinkedIn friend, and, when possible, give a second connection or a secondary reason for wanting to become a friend: "I heard you speak at the MPI conference…"

4. Always send a note when you accept someone as a Facebook friend or Twitter follower.

5. Be authentic, be real, and don't speak "corporatese".

6. Listen and look before you jump in and join a new community. It is clever young dogs that don't bound into an pack of old hounds, but spend some time sniffing…well, you know what.

7. Let people get to know you before you slip them your blog URL or Web site. (Remember the rules of dating!)

8. Remember, on the Web you ARE what you publish. Have something of value to say. It doesn't mean you have to be heavy every time you publish. You can be funny and on-topic, but have a thread of knowledge that you are trying to impart.

9. Encourage sharing. Re-tweet, but give credit. If you find something worthy of a good buzz, give it "word of mouse."

10. Questions beat out statements 60 to 1. People love to respond to questions, but don't do it every time. It gets annoying.

11. Listen. Then REALLY listen.

12. Ask leading questions; KEY questions that lead to more questions and more conversation.

13. Involve people in the decision-making. Online, this is by surveys and polls.

14. Bring interesting people to your page, not just interesting because of what they do.

15. Be positive and dynamic.

16. Mentor others.

17. Spend time remembering bits of information about other people. These bits of sometimes-trivial information make the other people feel important and special-even online.

18. Introduce key people to other key people.

19. Respond in a timely manner, be organized, and never seem too busy.

20. Deliver far more value than your fans expect.

It's important to note that some people use **multiple social media platforms** for engagement. Conversations are not limited to one platform.

Although it requires a little bit of research, it's often easy to create strong relationships when you connect with the same people on different social media platforms. It's like "oh, there you are again, good to see you."

For example, many people engage by sharing photos on Flickr, and they often share the links to their photos on Twitter or Facebook. They tag their photos so they show up on a Facebook News Feed.

The comments posted on these photos are also a great resource to help you find people to follow and grow your network. You can also do the same research with YouTube videos, Facebook pages, and any other social media platform your audience frequents. In addition, Foursquare and other geo-location applications are making it easier to create events and bring people together in person.

f: Engaging through Great Content:

To be successful in social media you need to be able to create good content in a conversational style. Good social media (a.k.a., conversational writing) is good journalistic writing with just a tad more personal approach added to it. A key would be to write as if the pyramid was inverted and always beginning by summarizing the conclusion.

One of the first things I learned about conversational writing came from Dr. Jakob Nielsen (http://www.slideshare.net/sheideman/writing-effectively-social-media-071608-3) as quoted in a slide share by Lisa Forner. He indicated that the first thing to learn about conversational writing is your reader. You, my dear reader, are not sitting down with a good book (God knows), but you **are searching** for information. Therefore, here is what Dr. Nielsen has to say about you:

- You have a short attention span. (Oops--lost you!)

- You are interactive by nature. (Better, put a link in...)

- You are a reader on a mission. (You may have found me through a search query, so I better put a lot of key words in my blog.)

Having read this, I now realize that my blog entries (often over 1,000 words) are way beyond your limited attention span. I write my blogs to be turned into books like this one, so they do tend to be too long in nature (sorry). "A wall of text is deadly for an interactive reader and is intimidating, boring and painful to read," says Dr Nielsen, and I agree with him.

A search about "conversational writing" brings up very little, but the search "social media writing" brings up many good tips, including these from Muhammad Saleem (http://www.copyblogger.com/writing-for-social-media/):

Start with the familiar: Introduce your article by drawing from a source that you think the social media audience will relate to and is interested in. Pop culture will often provide the perfect hook.

Introduce the unfamiliar: Once you've established a relationship with the reader by finding common ground, you can introduce your topic (i.e., the analysis or educational aspect of your article).

Connect the two: Once you have established common ground and introduced your insight, you need to connect the two. This makes your content not only easy to understand and digest for the readers, but also easy to remember and apply to their own lives.

Here is another excellent tip from Eric Brantner (http://digitallabz.com/blogs/10-foolproof-steps-to-writing-hot-social-media-content.html):

Be Conversational- The key word in social media is "social." Get rid of the stiff, boring content that lacks personality. Bring your readers into the conversation. Talk to the readers just as you would if you were sitting face to face. An interactive, personal tone will generate buzz for your content.

I would like to add a few suggestions of my own (don't moan):

- o Where possible write in the first person and speak directly to the reader (singular)

- o This next point is very unpopular but I am going to say it anyway (heretic):

- o Don't dumb down your writing unless you want dumb followers. English is a vast and rich language; use it.

- o Isn't a question often more powerful than a statement?

- o Précis, précis, précis (then shorten it).

- o What is your goal in writing the article?

- o Have you filled it with key words and have you completed a key word analysis?

- o Have you placed external links into the post?

- o Does your article grab the reader right away?

- o Is your content easy to absorb on the computer or smart phone screen? This could include:

- o Bullet points

- o Subheadings (search engines appreciate this to help with indexing as well as any reader being able to grasp the articles intention from an initial skim reading)

- o Interesting quotes

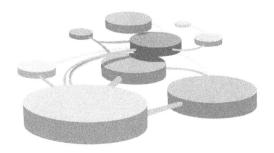

Secret Four:

How to Build a Winning Social Media Strategy

a) How to Develop a Social Media Strategy

If I were to take a SWAG (scientific wild ass guess), I would have to say that at least 40% of people using social media for the exposure of their brand are wasting a chunk of their hard work and money because they haven't developed a strategy.

Some of the content of this section comes from a great book (although very thick), called *The Social Media Bible*, by Lon Safko and David Brake (http://www.amazon.com/dp/0470411554/?tag=googhydr-20&hvadid=3349041931&ref=pd_sl_45evkre7jr_e).

In this book, the authors encourage you to think of your social media strategy as a platform supported by four pillars. You really need all four pillars to make your strategy work.

The four pillars are:

a) Communication

b) Collaboration

c) Education

d) Entertainment

You must keep in mind all four of these pillars as you create and activate your social media strategy.

Before we go too far down any one path, we should ask some questions:

• Are your customers likely to be online? Note that many people are online these days, but it might be that you have a product or service that isn't as frequently purchased or researched via the Web. What's your story?

• Are you ready to handle negativity? Platforms like blogs and videos allow for negative comments, and some company cultures aren't ready to engage with those opinions.

• How will you incorporate this into your staff's (or your own) workload? Are you willing to take on some interns and train them?

• How long are you willing to try it?

• What's your willingness to experiment, take risks, and adjust your plans?

• How will you measure results?

Just discovering those answers might tell you a bit about your business, whether or not you decide to go forward with building a strategy using social media tools.

Remember, it's a lot easier to NOT listen to customers and just blast your messages out with no regard as to how they're received but you're not reading this book looking for "easy" right? You're looking for "effective."

Strategy Starters:

If we're going to put a social media strategy into place, we need to align the path we're going to take, and develop it with an understanding of how to reach our goals. Where are we going? How are we going to get there? How do we know we've arrived? Here are 10 key actions to create a social media trategy:

1. **Communities:** Most social media strategies have to address several "communities of common interest," and dividing your customers (present and future) up into several well-defined communities that have common interests is important. Then, how will you encourage these communities to gather around your social media content? Since social media is part of public relations in marketing, we mustn't forget that there are seven publics in public relations and these can be used as guidelines as you look into your community structure:

o   Press (media) relations (don't forget bloggers)

o   Employee relations

o   Community relations

o   Educator relations

o   Consumer relations (*this is the biggie)

o   Stakeholder relations

o   Management relations

2. **Key Influencers**: From within these communities, list out, with full contact information, the key influencers. Those are the people who, if you help them understand who you are and what you do, may influence many others. This is the most time consuming part of developing a strategy, but also the most important. It is critical to note that it is an ongoing process and it should involve at least 10 new key people a day.

3. **Track down the top key influencers from each community and see what social media platforms they are using.** Also, don't forget that the key word in social networking is "networking." With programs like Facebook, MySpace, LinkedIn, etc., you can reach your key people by finding friends that you have in common. Then an introduction is easy.

4. **Spend several months just listening and seeing what the online conversations are all about.** Be a good little puppy and don't bound into the pack all slobbering with enthusiasm.

5. **Assign a Community Manager** (paid and with good writing skills) to become part of, and to handle, a community. It is best if the Community Manager has an interest in that particular community. From within the community, cultivate an "evangelist" (unpaid) to work with your Community Manager.

6. **Communications**: Create your social media platforms so that they will bring people to an understanding of who you are, what you know, and what you do; microblogs are commonly used to shout-out and point people to other information you want them to know about. The next step points to your blog, where you show your expertise and knowledge in a casual and friendly manner and certainly NOT in a sales-like manner. Blogs can also include vlogs, where you show your knowledge but on video (such as YouTube).

Once convinced of your expertise and thought leadership, these blogs and vlogs can point towards your Web site where finally consumers really understand what you have to offer.

Please understand that although this is an ideal progression, people will jump in at any one point and go on to another (if they are interested), so you must cross-reference your platforms at all points.

7. **Listening**: Implement rudimentary listening platforms such as Google Blogs or Technorati or others.

8. **Message**: Determine the message and the mix of content you intend to create for each community, and build a calendar around it. Remember your bottom line is to create "buzz." Learn how to build awareness and encourage conversations with the content you're creating.

9. **Measurement**: How are you going to measure your success or failure in the social media arena? Remember, it is not the ROI that counts in social media, it is the return on engagement (ROE). Here are some suggestions:

- Buzz, (conversations that go three or more in depth)

- Friends, followers, joiners, eyeballs

- Readers of your blogs

- Comments on your blogs

- Newsletter subscribers

- Unique Web site users that have come to your Web site from tweet links, blog links, etc.

- People who complete "conversion" activities on your Web site (You decide what those conversion activities are.)

10. **Test**: Try out your message with your peers and your consumers. Don't be afraid to ask, "What would you think if I said this….?"

b. Social Media Strategy Workbook

The following workbook asks all the questions you will need to actually create a Social Media Strategy. Find the answers and fill in the questions in the workbooks first:

HPR Social Media Strategy Workbook

Copyright 2010

1: How many communities are we trying to reach?

2: If we assigned a staff member to each community to listen and engage how many staff would we require?

3: How many staff hours per week are we able to devote to reaching these communities through social media?

4: Do we wish to network as well as broadcast?

5: If we wish to network, do we have or can we acquire a key influencer list for any of these communities? (See suggested Web sites to help find key influencers at the back of this workbook.)

6: Who will oversee the whole program?

7: Do we have information to communicate that would go well with platforms such as a blog or a vlog?

8: Do we have analytics on our Web site or Web page that can track our success?

9: If no to number 8, are we able to put analytics on our Web site or Web page?

10: How can we use social media to help complete our mission statement?

11: Which metrics do we want to use to measure our success in social media?

12: Who will you assign to report on the chosen metrics in #11?

13: From the URLs posted on the last couple of pages of this Workbook decide which platforms you are going to use to monitor your social media. (Monitoring and measuring are not the same).

14: To help develop your content calendar does your department have seasonal changes in activities or in your planning cycle? Are you willing to develop a content calendar? 15: What number of followers do we realistically hope to expect at the end of the fiscal year for each platform:
Facebook? _____ Twitter? _____ Blog Readership? _____
LinkedIn? _____ YouTube?_____ Flickr? _____

16: Do we already have a social media policy or do we need to develop one?

17: Who would chair a committee to develop a policy?

18: How can we use social media to improve inter-departmental understanding of what we do?

19: How can we use social media to improve our employees' understanding of what we do?

20: Will you promote your social media presence with logos and links from: Facebook, Twitter, LinkedIn, or blog on any of the following:

a) E-Newsletters
b) Direct Mail
c) Web page
d) Business cards
e) Letterhead
f) Flyers
g) Email

After completing this workbook you will have all the questions answered to create a full Social Media Strategy.

Here are two examples of short and simple strategies to guide the development of your own strategy:

HPR Social Media Strategy 2010-2011 (Sample Only)

Company Goals for Social Media:

HPR is a public relations coaching firm with heavy emphasis on social media and social networking. Our social media goals are to create a "buzz" that HPR is knowledgeable in PR and would be a good coaching partner to develop a social media strategy.

Company Objectives for Social Media:

HPR will obtain 5 speaking engagements and 7 new coaching clients through social media during the calendar year.

Communities of Common Interest:

HPR will become involved in the following communities (not in order of importance);

a) Destination Marketing Organizations

b) Lodging Associations

c) Restaurant Associations

d) Tourism Organizations

e) Speakers Guilds

f) Tourism industry bloggers and e-Zine publishers

g) PR Society of America

h) Other marketing experts in a similar position as myself who can back link to us

---

Key Influencer List:

HPR has developed a key influencer list of 172 people in each of the above communities (sorry, not available for public viewing). These will be added to on a daily basis.

The following social media platforms have been isolated as containing a majority of the people on the key influencer lists:

LinkedIn	114
Facebook	132
Twitter	74
My Space	12
Flickr	27
YouTube	7

The key influencer list also connects and names mutual "friends" for each of the key influencers. It also indicates that 42 of the key influencers do not have mutual friends on any of the platform and will need to be reached through other means.

Community Managers:

The following are assigned to be social media Community Managers because of their expertise and contacts within each of the communities listed:

John Hope-Johnstone: Destination Marketing
Organizations

Lodging Associations

Tourism Organizations

Other Marketing Experts:

Mary Gulch: Restaurant Association

Pete Hasbrock: New Media Programs
                                     Travel Industry Bloggers
                                     E-Zine

Zoya Bondaruk: Speaker Guilds
                                     Speaker Agents

Communication Platforms:

Relating to the numbers of key influencers found on each social media platform as listed above **HPR will** develop or expand its presence on the following social media platforms:

a)   Facebook fan page

b)   LinkedIn

c)   Twitter

d)   Buzz Master Blog

e)   YouTube: Cheap Video Production Channel

We will make sure that all of our platforms provide a link and a progression to move the reader into a deeper understanding of **HPR** and our expertise. Moving from microblogs such as; Twitter, Facebook, LinkedIn, to macroblogs, vlogs and Podcasts.

Media Content Calendar and Key Words:

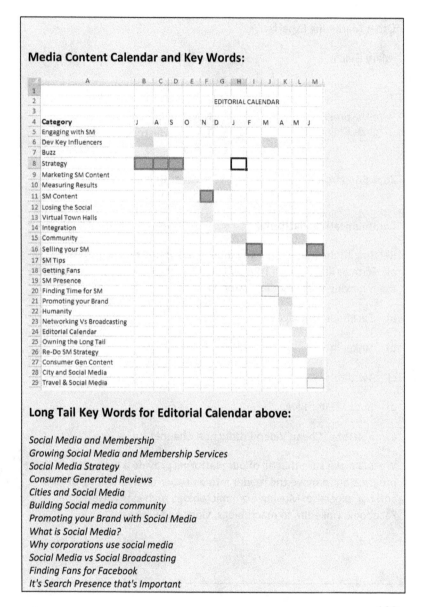

	A	B	C	D	E	F	G	H	I	J	K	L	M
1													
2								EDITORIAL CALENDAR					
3													
4	**Category**	J	A	S	O	N	D	J	F	M	A	M	J
5	Engaging with SM												
6	Dev Key Influencers												
7	Buzz												
8	Strategy												
9	Marketing SM Content												
10	Measuring Results												
11	SM Content												
12	Losing the Social												
13	Virtual Town Halls												
14	Integration												
15	Community												
16	Selling your SM												
17	SM Tips												
18	Getting Fans												
19	SM Presence												
20	Finding Time for SM												
21	Promoting your Brand												
22	Humanity												
23	Networking Vs Broadcasting												
24	Editorial Calendar												
25	Owning the Long Tail												
26	Re-Do SM Strategy												
27	Consumer Gen Content												
28	City and Social Media												
29	Travel & Social Media												

Long Tail Key Words for Editorial Calendar above:

Social Media and Membership
Growing Social Media and Membership Services
Social Media Strategy
Consumer Generated Reviews
Cities and Social Media
Building Social media community
Promoting your Brand with Social Media
What is Social Media?
Why corporations use social media
Social Media vs Social Broadcasting
Finding Fans for Facebook
It's Search Presence that's Important

Objectives:
Facebook fan page: 500 fans by year end
LinkedIn: 300 Invites accepted by year-end
Buzz Master Blog: 100 readers per day average.
YouTube: 100 subscribers to channel
Our Website: 5,000 hits per month and 2,000 unique users
E-New Opt-Ins: 300 subscribers to Tsunami Report
Seminars: 15
Long Term clients: 9

Social Media Strategic Plan 2 (Sample Only)
XYZ Athletic Club
Year 2010-2011
September 30 2010 to September 30 2011

1: Company Goals for Social Media:

"To create an online community containing information and conversations about health, fitness and fun for Corvallis residents of all ages."

2: Company Objectives for Social Media: Using the Value Added landing page on the Web site to have 80 new prospects download the free trial membership by September 30 2011.Total growth of hits on the Web site from social media platforms as shown in the analytics in percentage over last year to be 25%. This percentage increase of hits to the Club's Web site will be composed of numerical increases from the following social media platforms by September 30 2011:

Facebook   650 new fans

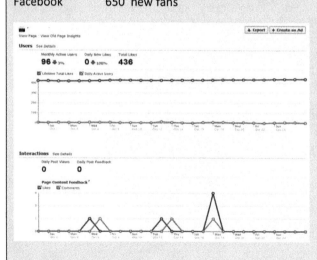

E: Twitter   300 followers (www.twittercounter.com, mine)

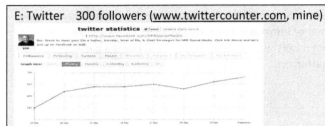

F: Blog: Average 100 reads per month (Blog stats chart below (mine))
WordPress provides.

G: LinkedIn: 5,000 connections (although companies can now have
Linked in corporate pages on Linkedin, for smaller organizations I still
recommend keeping it more personal.

 H: YouTube: 1000 views (Short video clips from department heads).

3: Define your Communities of Common Interest:

Group Exercise

2) Activities (Gym, Leagues, Runners)

3) Aquatics

4) Children's activities

5) Racquet Sports

6) Weight Loss and Fitness

7) Membership

8) Club Socials

9) Community relations

10) Media relations

4: Survey which Social Media Platforms your Communities are using (either formal or informal). In a very informal survey I have concluded that those members who are involved in social media a using the following platforms:

Linked in	X
Facebook	X
Twitter	X
You Tube	X
Blog	X

5: Community Managers:
The following are suggested to be social media Community Managers because of their expertise and contacts within each of the communities listed:

1) Group Exercise,	Pete
2) Activities (Gym, Leagues, Runners)	Harry
3) Aquatics	Susan
4) Children's Activities	Suze
5) Racquet Sports	John
6) Weight Loss and Fitness	Pete2
7) Membership	Sam
8) Club Socials	Vicky
9) Community Relations	Mary
10) Media Relations	Chuck

All of the above should have Admin status on Facebook.

6: Media Content Calendar and Key Words: Each Community Manager needs to contribute to a content calendar that will drive the information you post on your blog, Twitter, or on your Facebook page. This can be seasonally driven or by your own calendar of events:

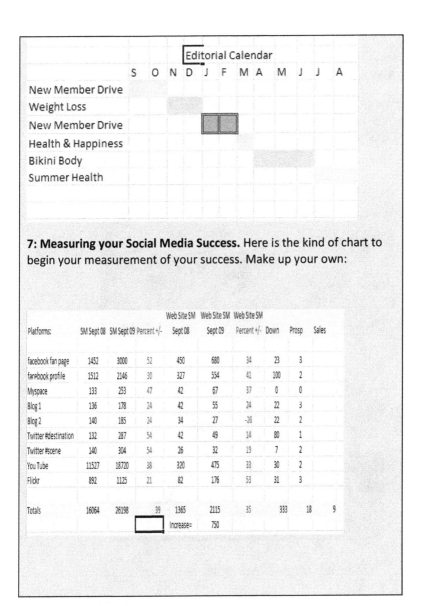

	S	O	N	D	J	F	M	A	M	J	J	A
Editorial Calendar												
New Member Drive												
Weight Loss												
New Member Drive												
Health & Happiness												
Bikini Body												
Summer Health												

7: Measuring your Social Media Success. Here is the kind of chart to begin your measurement of your success. Make up your own:

Platforms:	SM Sept 08	SM Sept 09	Percent +/-	Web Site SM Sept 08	Web Site SM Sept 09	Web Site SM Percent +/-	Down	Prosp	Sales
facebook fan page	1452	3000	52	450	680	34	23	3	
facebook profile	1512	2146	30	327	554	41	100	2	
Myspace	133	253	47	42	67	37	0	0	
Blog 1	136	178	24	42	55	24	22	3	
Blog 2	140	185	24	34	27	-26	22	2	
Twitter #destination	132	287	54	42	49	14	80	1	
Twitter #scene	140	304	54	26	32	19	7	2	
You Tube	11527	18720	38	320	475	33	30	2	
Flickr	892	1125	21	82	176	53	31	3	
Totals	16064	26198	39	1365	2115	35	333	18	9
				Increase=	750				

8: Welcome Page for Facebook:

We recommend that a Welcome page be created on the Facebook page for first-time users where they would land before they click the "Like" button. You could follow something similar in format to HPR's:

This page is all about conversation and sharing. I hope that you will find it

Secret Five:

You won't know if you're Winning or not Without Good Metrics

Targeting and measuring objectives is the first step to alignment. Here is what mature social media marketers are trying to accomplish and measure with their social media campaigns:

1. Increase Web traffic   88%

2. Increase lead generation   75%

3. Increase sales revenues   71%

4. Improve SEO   69%

5. Improve brand awareness   54%

6. Reduce customer acquisition costs 45%

7. Improve Public Relations   44%

8. Improve customer support quality 36%

9. Improve customer support costs   32%

a.Starting Your Social Media Report:

To be effective with your social media campaign you need to be able to measure and prove that your marketing efforts have increased the number of friends, followers, or subscribers in social media, and that they are adding to the number of unique users of your brand's Web site. If this can't be proven, then I would suggest that the social media effort will someday be in trouble. You must prove that you create a positive effect on the bottom line.

All Result in Increased Web site Traffic

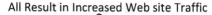

Macro Blog, V Logs
Podcasts, Readers,
Viewers, Listeners all
driving people to the Web site

Micro-Blogs, Social Platforms
Friends, Fans Followers
drive people towards
the Macro-Blogs

At the bottom of your reporting pyramid are the lower tier statistics: How many communities? How many friends on Facebook? How many followers on Twitter or subscribers on YouTube? How many key influencers have become friends and how many of your messages have they followed?

All of the above stats are important indicators of the success of your social media efforts. However, if social media is to survive in the corporate world, the hungry beasts known as "number crunchers" must be satisfied and I don't think feeding them a steady diet of the above campaign numbers alone is going to satisfy their insatiable appetite.

In the corporate world, any business activity that is not part of a sale is fluff....yes, fluff! Marketing is **any** business activity that affects the transfer of goods, products, or services, forget this at your own peril.

In this book we have stated often that social media really belongs under the heading of Public relations and yet, not one marketing department should own a monopoly on social media.

However, even Public relations must answer to the beastly number crunchers and show that positive third party comments that drive people to your Web site and finally (hopefully) to a sale are valuable to the bottom line. Does this mean that every tweet must contain your Web site URL? Definitely NOT, only a portion!

After you drive them from your social media to your Web site, the question of how many people convert after visiting your Web site is a whole other story, and most likely is someone else's responsibility.

Now, I am cute, but not stupid (well, not too stupid). I know that people don't follow logical paths in social media; they randomly snack on all the content. Still, it makes sense to think of social media as a logical pathway as you herd your faithful followers up the path to your point of sale--which is your brand Web site.

Therefore, to be effective with your social media campaign, the increased number of friends, followers or subscribers should be affecting the number of unique users of your brand Web site as recorded by your Web analytics.

Top 30 of 76 Total Referrers		
#	Hits	Referrer
1	90 1.53%	http://www.facebook.com/HPRSocialMedia
2	15 0.25%	http://www.google.com/search
3	14 0.24%	http://www.google.com/url
4	8 0.14%	http://www.facebook.com/
5	8 0.14%	http://www.facebook.com/l.php
6	6 0.10%	http://www.prweb.com/releases/2010/01/prweb3407584.htm
7	3 0.05%	http://www.facebook.com/reqs.php
8	3 0.05%	http://www.prod.facebook.com/HPRSocialMedia
9	2 0.03%	http://buzzmaster.wordpress.com/

As you can see from my Web site analytics (chart above), the majority of the top 9 referrers come from my social media platforms and my blog.

This will not be so obvious with a larger brand site...but social media platforms and blogs should show in the analytics, although perhaps further down the list.

b. Social Media Monthly Statement (Example)

Value Statement:

The social media department increased followers by 23%, which drove 2,700 new users on the brand site over the past 30 days. Using the standard 20% conversion rate for the site, this means that the social media department increased sales by a possible 540 units at an average of $720 per unit resulting in $388,800 in revenue.

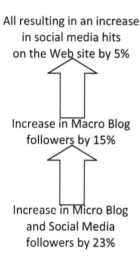

All resulting in an increase
in social media hits
on the Web site by 5%

Increase in Macro Blog
followers by 15%

Increase in Micro Blog
and Social Media
followers by 23%

The page following the above summary page would contain the analytics from your micro-blogs and macro-blogs and Web site that support the above value statement and pyramid.

Platforms:	SM Sept 08	SM Sept 09	Percent +/-	Web Site SM Sept 08	Web Site SM Sept 09	Web Site SM Percent +/-	Down	Prosp	Sales
facebook fan page	1452	3000	52	450	680	34	23	3	
facebook profile	1512	2146	30	327	554	41	100	2	
Myspace	133	253	47	42	67	37	0	0	
Blog 1	136	178	24	42	55	24	22	3	
Blog 2	140	185	24	34	27	-26	22	2	
Twitter #destination	132	287	54	42	49	14	80	1	
Twitter #scene	140	304	54	26	32	19	7	2	
You Tube	11527	18720	38	320	475	33	30	2	
Flickr	892	1125	21	82	176	53	31	3	
Totals	16064	26198	39	1365	2115	35	333	18	9
				Increase=	750				

Now, you have a "Value Statement" and you have shown the increase in the numbers that drive people to the mother ship (Web site) and how many convert into a sale.

You will now need to show your Web site analytics and find the numbers for each of the social media platforms, and verify your statements that social media IS driving visits to your Web site.

c. Monitoring Social Media Performance:

Monitoring and measuring might seem to be the same, but they are not. Monitoring warns us of dangers that must be avoided. Measuring allows us to estimate, by comparison, if we are getting ahead or falling behind our objectives. In this section we are going to chat about monitoring.

There are literally hundreds of social media monitoring programs out there. They are task-oriented search engines that present their information using different dashboards. Like so many monitoring devices, including our bathroom scales, it is **not** how perfectly the scale reports your weight's gain or loss, but the fact that you use the same scale to weigh yourself each time you step on it, so you know if you are going up or down. (See appendix for list of monitoring URLs.)

Specialized Social Media Markets

At **HPR** in addition to our general business seminars, we also build specialized social media marketing models for different industry requirements such as follows:

a) **"Social Media for Growing and Retaining Membership,"** which is highly valuable for membership-driven organizations such as associations, health clubs, etc.

b) **"Social Media for City Governments."** Cities have their own set of challenges dealing with social media, but they all realize the need to communicate more openly and effectively with their citizens.

c) **"Social Media for Sales,"** which is perfect for any organization with a sales department.

d) **"Social Media for Hospitality and Tourism."** A great seminar for any organization involved in the hospitality and tourism industry.

a: Social Media for Growing and Retaining Membership

This section is important for membership-based organizations such as associations, Chambers of Commerce, Destination Marketing Organizations, etc., however it also pertains to organizations wishing to maintain good customer relations, or charities and not-for-profits wishing to maintain or increase their donor base.

Membership-based organizations exist to serve their members. People join membership-based organizations to gain professional status, update their education, network with others, grow their business, and to monitor profession-related policy positions that could affect their business.

All of the above reasons for joining a membership-based organization depend on the sharing of information and the building and maintenance of networks. With the aging of the population and the old guard slowly leaving the workplace, it is interesting to find social media tools are not necessarily considered the most effective in reaching membership goals. In fact, the most effective social networking tools are considered to be those that are housed within the organization itself, namely LISTSERV (50%) and/or a private association social network (39%). It is difficult to know if this response is due to entitlement in these platforms, because, except in odd cases, I have rarely found in-house list servers or social networks to be well used.

Approximately two-thirds of association respondents report still using snail-mail welcome kits in 2010. This is a 15 percent decrease from 2009 (68% in 2010 versus 83% in 2009). However, findings indicate that associations with greater than 80% renewals are significantly more likely to use the mailed welcome kits (75% versus 58%). The question for some associations might be, if your membership is aging and no fresh blood is coming in, are you fishing where the fish are?

I am not advocating giving up tried and true methods of recruiting and retaining membership or donors. I **am** suggesting that social media, if done effectively, can increase the satisfaction level of present members or donors by increasing the perceived value. It will increase the potential renewal and referral rates. It can slowly become part of your membership services campaign but should, like the other methods of recruitment, be monitored and gauged for its effectiveness.

Here are 10 steps to developing and retaining members using social media:

1. Assess what is working and what is not by the actual number of members each social media platform brings in. Do the same exercise with old methods of membership solicitation, and don't allow sacred cows to remain just because some board member ten years ago had the idea.
2. Begin your foray into social media for membership building and retention with a poll to see which social media platforms the majority of the present members utilize. Is it Facebook (most likely)? or LinkedIn? Do they use Twitter? Blog?
3. Go for the low hanging fruit. This includes your lapsed members and your non-member users. They've already expressed an interest in your organization, so now is the time to convey how important membership is for their own success in today's world. Search for them on social media sites using a Customer Relationship Management (CRM) system such as Batchbook.com (http://batchblue.com/product-info.html) which allows you to see which social media platforms your prospects are using.
4. Once you locate a lapsed member on, say, LinkedIn, then see which active members are connected to him/her and have them contact the lapsed member via the social media platform in a social manner and bring them back into the fold.
5. If you decide to develop a Facebook fan page for membership, you must ask the question, "WHY?". Why would a prospective

member go to this page? What are you going to offer that is special and will drive them to visit that page? What special information is going to be on it to make members go? Also, don't forgo your own or other staff members' regular Facebook profile pages. I gain far more social capital and conversations from my regular Facebook profile page than my business fan page. That doesn't mean you should overload your profile page with business stuff, just keep it social. Let people know who you are and where you work.

6. Twitter is a "news agency" and it works best for broadcast informational purposes. It is great at conferences to help people find people, to update any changes in program, and to point members towards special information you are putting out about the conference. A hash tag is a great way to get groups together.

7. Don't forget about YouTube. Short video clips about presentations at a conference are a great way to remind people who didn't go what a great time and a great educational opportunity they are missing. Also pulling the videos into your Web site is great content and search engines love them.

8. Don't forget good social media is all about the quality of your content and information. If you just blah blah blah, then people will move on. If you give them key information or point them in the direction of good content via a link, they will come back for more.

9. It is all about getting people involved and not feeling that an organization is elitist. This is especially important to young prospective members, who may think it's just an old boy/girl network, and that they will not feel welcome.

10. It is all about giving your organization a face and a voice, and by that, I don't mean one face but many.

b) Social Media for City Governments

While elected officials have been relatively quick to pounce upon the power of social media as a communications tool (after President Obama paved the way), city governments have not been quick to adopt the new media to stay in touch with their citizens. In July 2009, a Fels Institute of Government (http://www.fels.upenn.edu/) survey found that only 50% of the 79 cities surveyed had a Facebook presence, while 56% were on Twitter.

A highly unscientific study by our own organization, (using a Facebook search: "City of"), could find only six U.S. cities with a Facebook fan page. More cities had "unofficial Facebook pages" created by non-profits, perhaps with the blessing of the city, perhaps not. There also seems to be an organization running around putting up Facebook template pages for cities, all with very similar content. The three cities we found that had these templates were: Sacramento, San Diego, and Brampton, California. Each had only a few followers.

These unofficial city fan pages market themselves as "Company", and they designate themselves as "Community Pages," and all begin with, "Our goal is to make this Community Page the best collection of shared knowledge on this topic. If you have a passion for **XYZ City**, sign up and we'll let you know when we're ready for your help. You can also get us started by suggesting a relevant Wikipedia article or the Official Site."

One of the first official city pages we found was Albany, Oregon (http://www.facebook.com/cityofalbany?ref=ts), which has a fan page following of over 600 people, considering the city's populations of about 49,000 people - is very good.

Albany seems to use its posts mainly to announce job openings, Parks and Recreation programs, and event announcements. It does allow fans to write on its wall and all of them seem to be of a positive nature.

The City of Philadelphia has a series of unofficial Facebook pages, and one "non-profit" page with about 120,000 followers. The page has good content for events and festivals and enjoys good participation.

Another good example of a city site is the City and County of San Francisco with 257,000 fans.

The City and County of San Francisco do not seem to allow fan contributions on their pages, but they use it as a one-way communications tool to announce meetings, alerts, and special events. With just under 250,000 fans it is a popular site. The page owners are classified as an "organization." It looks like an official page but when we tried the phone number, we got what sounded like a fax machine.

There appears to be multiple reasons cities drag their feet in their development of social media, according to the Fels Institute Report. These reasons include concerns about the potential for public criticism, legal issues, workload, and general cost to the often cash-strapped towns. However, the benefits of social media outreach, according to the researchers at Penn State, outweigh the potential downsides.

In speaking to the Fels Institute, the City of Philadelphia's then-Assistant Managing Director Jeff Friedman, said, "The value for us is being able to reach so many people at one time at zero cost. Again, we are such a big organization and there is so much going on. Certainly we feel as a part of this administration we are doing a great deal of fantastic, transformational work and that we need to get this out to people." ("Making the Most of Social Media: 7 Lessons From Successful Cities," 2010, http://www.fels.upenn.edu/news/making-most-social-media.)

Cities are rushing to prepare policies and procedures that they hope will help them ease gracefully into the social media world. In many cases, they are so draconian that any employee would be foolish to attempt to tweet about a departmental activity without going through the legal department first.

Seattle has a good social media policy (http://www.cityofseattle.net/pan/SocialMediaPolicy.htm), and encourages the rank-and-file of city employees to communicate, where appropriate, using social media. In their preamble to the policy, they state, "To address the fast-changing landscape of the Internet and the way residents communicate and obtain information online, City of Seattle departments may consider using social media tools to reach a broader audience. The City encourages the use of social media to further the goals of the City and the missions of its departments, where appropriate."

Seattle divides social media use into two categories:

1. As channels for disseminating time-sensitive information. Example: emergency information. (Usually Twitter is used.)
2. As marketing/promotional channels that increase the City's ability to broadcast its messages to the widest possible audience. (Facebook and Blogs)

The City of Seattle clearly outlines what is acceptable from the public and recommends that all posts from the public that do not meet these standards be removed:

Users and visitors to social media sites shall be notified that the intended purpose of the site is to serve as a mechanism for communication between City departments and members of the public. City of Seattle social media site articles and comments containing any of the following forms of content shall not be allowed:

1. Comments not topically related to the particular social medium article being commented upon;
2. Comments in support of or in opposition to political campaigns or ballot measures;
3. Profane language or content;
4. Content that promotes, fosters, or perpetuates discrimination on the basis of race, creed, color, age, religion, gender, marital status, status with regard to public assistance, national origin, physical or mental disability or sexual orientation;
5. Sexual content or links to sexual content;
6. Solicitations of commerce;
7. Conduct or encouragement of illegal activity;
8. Information that may tend to compromise the safety or security of the public or public systems; or
9. Content that violates a legal ownership interest of any other party.

Cities are also concerned about individual state laws regarding record retention. Therefore, it is always advisable that a back-link be provided to an expanded version of the social media post hosted on the city's main Web site, where the body of work should be maintained for legal purposes.

City Twitter accounts seem to be limited to information of a critical nature where city departments need to get information out quickly. Police, fire, and emergency departments are using Twitter.

Facebook is being used for less-immediate city information, such as job openings, events, department notifications, and celebrations. Content that cannot be retrieved from Facebook via an application-programming interface (API), and needs to be retained as a record, is being printed and maintained according to the city's records retention policy.

Some smaller cities have used social media to help give city government a face. By city government, I mean city departments. YouTube, Flickr, and podcasts have been used to explain the workings of certain projects, and the departments themselves, and different employees have taken on the task of making city government departments more human.

Many city governments are using the White House template (http://www.whitehouse.gov/open/documents/open-government-directive) for social media, the "Open Government Directive". Others are using the Microsoft program "Open Government" (http://www.microsoft.com/industry/government/guides/Gov20.aspx) to become more transparent while still keeping within the myriad of regulations that surround a city. Although designed for the federal government it has many good concepts for other forms of government wishing to enter the social media arena as well.

The social media platforms most commonly used by cities are:

1. Facebook, for postings about such things as parks and recreation activities, upcoming meetings, special events, or job openings.
2. Twitter, which is being used very effectively as a fast communications tool by police, fire departments, roads departments, and 911 responses.

3. YouTube, to help explain departmental activities either to the public or for new employees.

We believe that social media can assist with city communications in the following ways:

o   Improved transparency of information
o   Improved responsiveness to citizen needs
o   Improved citizen engagement in planning and strategy

For example, the Phoenix police department produces a daily vlog entitled "The Last 24" (http://www.cityofphoenix.org/police/last24.html), reporting on crimes, tragedies, and the progress of standing cases. This is a huge public relations tool (in the positive sense) for the police department of Phoenix, since it shows them progressing with cases. It also gives a human face and humanity to what can often be seen as just a uniform.

The City of Boston has designed an iPhone app (http://www.psfk.com/2009/07/boston-debuts-citizen-connect-iphone-app.html) in an effort to streamline some of its governmental bureaucracy, allowing citizens to report complaints-ranging from broken street lights and potholes to graffiti and downed power lines-directly to City Hall. After filing a complaint, users will receive a tracking number so that they can easily follow-up if the problem persists.

Governments are increasingly seeing social media not as a Pandora's box never to be opened, but as an opportunity to meet their obligations in truly new ways.

Social media falls under the marketing tool of public relations, and more specifically communications. We all sell something. It is inherent in our existence. City departments sell different things according to their mission statements, but largely, cities as a whole sell the fact that they are being responsive to their citizens, and are doing the best job possible in fulfilling their citizens' needs.

When cities fail to do this, the gap of disbelief widens between the citizenry and the city. If this happens, then often when the city requires a vote on a levy or tax increase, it will be voted down. In this instance, the items are voted down NOT because the citizens don't understand the measure (which they may not), but because they don't trust or understand the government.

The bottom line for cities is about the same as non-governmental organizations:

1. City Facebook fan pages will be populated mostly by people who in the commercial world would be considered "clients". You have to work at expanding the reach further than preaching to the converted.
2. Twitter followers are younger and are looking for something new: new information, gossip, actions, or events. If your department doesn't really have anything exciting to say or to highlight (and this doesn't mean you aren't doing a great job), then maybe Twitter isn't for you. Departments that want fast response will employ Twitter successfully.
3. Blogs deliver "thought leadership;" they give the reader reason to believe that this department knows what it's doing, be it park management, road repair, transportation, senior citizen involvement, or overall government. It shows why people should believe you know what you are doing.
4. YouTube, Flickr, and podcasts are great tools to explain departmental activities and progress on a project, especially if they are pulled into the city's Web site.

d) Social Media for Sales Prospecting

Much has been written about Internet marketing, social media, and sales prospecting. Early blogs commented that social media was of "little" or "no" value to sales. Later, blogs said there's "maybe a little" value. Now blogs are beginning to say that Internet marketing and social media fit nicely into the sales funnel.

You'll note that we use the term "Internet marketing" and not just social media alone. Why? Social media is only one part of Internet marketing. Other parts are e-mail marketing, SEOs, SEM, Internet affiliate marketing, and many more. They don't work well separately but together they rock! The following chart, abstracted from the wonderful folks at **Advanced Media Productions** advmediaProductions.com, shows the full scope of Internet marketing:

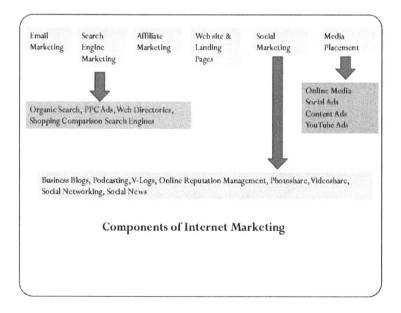

Components of Internet Marketing

As you can see, the Internet has developed into a range of marketing tools far more diverse than just social media. Yet the term "Internet marketing" is not widely used. The Internet marketing tool that best supports the sales effort depends on the type of sales. If you are involved in online e-tail sales, or a brick-and-mortar shop, then e-mail, SEM, affiliate marketing, and social media are all definitely valuable Internet marketing tools, because you are trying to drive people into your retail shop or onto your e-tail site.

If you are in a sales process involving a product or service requiring a face-to-face meeting with a prospect, and possibly the negotiation of an agreement, then you would most likely benefit from e-mail campaigns, a landing capture page, and social marketing.

> **As all salespeople know, prospecting is the very lifeblood of good sales. Prospecting is the forte of one particular social media platform: LinkedIn. This platform is not for every type of sales, but it covers many, such as services and higher ticket items.**

Let me walk you through how LinkedIn can be used as a prospecting tool. My occupation is giving half- and full-day seminars on social media, all over the country and internationally. I present them to corporations as well as associations, governments, and non-profit organizations. When I am not presenting seminars, I am often prospecting for new clients.

I begin by looking for a company, organization, association, or government agency with which I may have a potential relationship. In this demonstration, I will use Four Seasons Hotels. I worked for them back in the 1970s (best company I ever worked for, I might add). In addition, I have held social media seminars for other hotel companies, and therefore can provide testimonials.

Four Seasons Hotels' business mix is largely corporate travel, and therefore I am guessing that a high percentage of their clients are already involved in social media.

Step one is to see if they are listed on LinkedIn as a corporation. It would make life much easier if they were. Go to LinkedIn's search bar, click on the pull down, and choose "companies," then type in the company you are looking for. If they are listed then you can find the name of the right individual to turn into a prospect.

Once you have located a suitable prospect, you can find out if you have any contacts in common. This is where LinkedIn excels and a little effort goes a long, long way. I have only 199 connections, but they could connect me to nearly two million people.

Once we have found a suitable prospect (in this case the unnamed regional VP for the West Coast), it is a matter of finding someone to introduce us. If you have ever tried today to get someone you don't know to return a phone call, an email, a letter, or to see you in person if you cold call them, you will know that it is almost impossible. People are so busy and with so many avenues to bombard them, they hunker down in their bomb shelters and it is very difficult to get through to them.

So now, I go back to LinkedIn and check to see if the regional VP and myself have any friends in common. Of my nearly two million possible connections, surely someone knows this person. Low and behold there is! (I have again obscured his/her name for the sake of privacy). Better still, it is a first generation contact-someone I know personally.

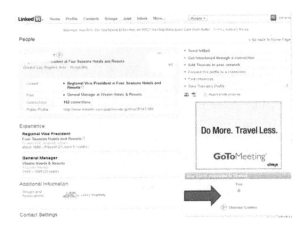

Now we have three choices:

1. Contact the regional VP directly through LinkedIn, mention the friend in common, cc the friend, hoping that he/she will intercede for me or

2. Email the friend from LinkedIn to ask his or her help in contacting the regional VP. After all, just because they show up as knowing each other, it doesn't mean they like each other.

3. Add one more step to the process and do a Google search on the regional VP, which will show the other social media that he or she is using. Visit those social media platforms for more insight into the VP. I tend to like to do a little more research by the name of the prospect to see what other social media platforms he/she is on, or to see what press releases, articles, speeches, or honors the person might have recently received or given.

4. Having completed this quick side step, I go back to our friend in common and send him/her a direct message from LinkedIn asking if he/she would send an email introducing the regional VP and myself.

5. Once the introduction e-mail goes out, wait a few days. Then, send your own email to the prospect with a copy (cc) to your sponsor thanking him or her for the introduction. I would suggest starting the subject line of the email with the first name of the person (on the East coast use the last name), and it might read as follows, "Bill, regarding the introduction from Tom Zyler."

6. Keep the tone of the email light and friendly. Don't hit him/her with heavy sales pitches. Give a short line or two as to how you know Tom, and how kind it is of him to take the time to introduce the two of you.

7. Let the prospect know what you do and that you would like to see if it might be a good fit for (in this case) Four Seasons Hotels. Give the prospect a link to your Web site, blog, and other information where he can flesh out who you are and what you know. If you have other contacts in common this is a good time to mention them. In addition, if you found out any recent awards or activities regarding the prospect in your Google research and subsequent social media follow-up, this is a nice time to mention it.

8. Inform the prospect that you will contact them within a week or so to get their "help" in seeing if your service or product will be a good "fit" for their organization, and ask if they would take your call.

9. This system of prospecting using social media works for me time and time again. You will have to refine it to suit your style. If you don't have a LinkedIn account, then it will take a short while to build up the connections required for good prospecting, but certainly no longer than three or four months.

d: Social Media for Hospitality and Tourism

The tourism industry was one of the first to see the value of the Web site and the value of search engine optimization and they have been quick to respond to the possibilities of social media. However, social media is more confusing and ethereal to many destination marketing managers because of its many facets and the time commitment on limited staff availability.

The Web Site, in its early days, could be easily understood by destination marketers as it was looked upon as being an on-line brochure, (of course it evolved into being much more). However Social Media is so new and has such great potential that there is nothing in the past to which we can relate.

The question is not how "WE" can use social media to attract visitors? It is how "THEY" (the visitor) are already using Internet marketing to find us and Social Media to help with their decision-making process.

Wikipedia defines social media as being part of "social validation". Social validation , or social proofing, is a psychological phenomenon that occurs in ambiguous situations when people do not have enough information to make opinions independently and instead look for external clues like popularity, third-party endorsements, friends and family, to develop that level of trust.

If we accept this definition then we have to pose the question; when are people requiring the largest dose of external validation about their travel choices? If we find this tipping point then we have found when the largest number of travelers will be using social media.

Social validation is required less for familiar destinations, to locations where we vacate regularly. We don't need our choices to be validated to go to these places, unless a new sub-choice has to be made; like a new restaurant or a new event. This will be true of shorter vacations within 50 to 100 miles from home.

We would require far more social media input and validation for going to a far away land where we have never been before and where the language and customs are different. It is also a big YES for trips that require a lot of planning and contain a lot of stops, like a long road trip, even though the road trip may visit our own country, with familiar customs, (except for some odd states) and common currency. It is also a big YUP for special occasion vacations where the pressure is on to make it perfect, like a honeymoon, or a big family reunion.

Planning a long distance trip where social validation is required can be a nightmare. Here are some creative ways that tourism agencies are helping to overcome these obstacles. One of the first lessons we need to remember is that facebook NOT Google is the number one search engine. More people complete a search on facebook than on Google!!

In a recent blog post by Sarah Chong she gives an excellent example of a trip to Japan and how very useful she found the Visit Japan 2010 facebook page that aggregates all the travel info and links you'll ever need! The layout is clean and information is organized. "It's the first place (not Google!) I would go to when planning for a Japan trip," she says. Get updates through the facebook page, ask questions and share your experiences with others. Who would you trust more, the tips and views of a fellow tourist or the tourism board?

Below is a screen shot of the visitjapan2010 facebook page. We have to be careful about losing the social of social media. Are we tricking out our facebook pages to look take over our Web site pages, that is NOT their purpose. Their purpose is to bring people together for a conversation about the product or service. To give them social validation, not to replicate something we already have.

Having said that doesn't mean that a little more information is a bad thing. Just don't make it into a second Web site. You will lose the whole meaning of social media.

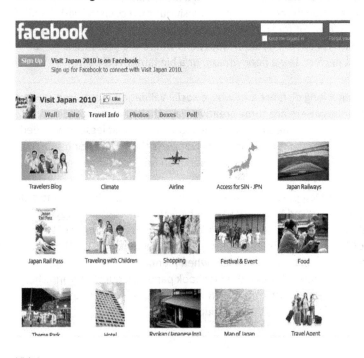

Visit Japan

New Zealand also uses a nicely branded YouTube channel promoting their brand "The Youngest Country on Earth". It not only shows you great videos, it helps you plan your trip as well! The channel links you to information about New Zealand, getting to New Zealand, places to stay, and a New Zealand map answering all the scary questions a traveler may need to know.

We still pose the question, is a slick professional video what the "social media" inquirer is looking for in their social validation. It's a lovely dream piece and it is aimed at the folks who are still thinking about going to New Zealand while the social media consumer has **already** made up their minds and are looking to validate a decision already made.

Sometimes our videos can be too slick, too professional whereas a video done with a flip by a tourist from the home country, ooing and aahing, might be much more effective.

To give them credit they do have a <u>Have Your Say</u> section way down at the bottom of the page, where tourists tape a video postcard and tell their story this adds to the social validation.

New Zealand

There is another thought to be pondered. My son sent me a very well produced video by the Scotland Tourist Board on Edinburgh. He sent it to me NOT to validate his decision to move to Edinburgh, but for bragging rights to the family. Well produced, high quality, videos have two important roles, as a dream factory and for bragging rights.

Tourism and Consumer-Generated Review Sites

In 1995 when Amazon.com first began letting customers publish reviews of products, many people, myself included, thought the Internet retailer had lost their collective marbles. Letting consumers rant about products in public was a recipe for retail suicide, we thought. Now, almost 15 years later, customer reviews are as common as hyperlinks, and a retail Web site that does not have feedback loops is considered irrelevant. In fact, more than 5 million consumers have submitted tens of millions of reviews on Amazon.com.

Do consumer-generated reviews affect business? Yes, reports the Nielsen Company in a July 2009 study of 25,000 consumers in 50 countries. Ninety percent of consumers surveyed noted that they trust recommendations from people they know, while 70 percent trusted consumer opinions offered online.

Jonathan Carson, President of Online, International, for the Nielsen Company, (http://en-us.nielsen.com) said, "The explosion in Consumer Generated Media over the last couple of years means consumers' reliance on word of mouth in the decision-making process, either from people they know or online consumers they don't, has increased significantly."

The 2009 report uses this graph to illustrate some degree of trust in the following forms of advertising:

Recommendations from friends   90%
Consumer opinions   70%
Brand Websites   70%
Editorial Content   69%
TV   62%
Newspapers   61%
Search Engine Results Ads   41%
Online banner ads   33%
Nielson Trust in Advertising 2009

Back in 2007, comScore, Inc., a leader in measuring the digital world, announced the results of a study conducted with The Kelsey Group, a leading research and strategic analysis firm focused on local media and advertising, that examined the impact of consumer-generated reviews on the price consumers were willing to pay for a service delivered offline. The study, based on a survey of more than 2,000 U.S. Internet users in October 2007, revealed that consumers were willing to pay at least 20% more for services receiving an "Excellent" or 5-star rating than for the same service receiving a "Good" or 4-star rating.

The study reported the non-Internet sales impact of online reviews for restaurants, hotels, travel, legal, medical, automotive, and home services. Nearly one out of every four Internet users (24%) reported using online reviews prior to paying for a service delivered offline. Of those who consulted an online restaurant review, 41% subsequently visited the restaurant, while 40% of those who read a hotel review subsequently stayed at the hotel.

More than three-quarters of review users in nearly every category reported that the review had a significant influence on their purchase, with hotels ranking the highest (87%). Ninety-seven percent of those surveyed who said they made a purchase based on an online review said they found the review to have been accurate. Review users also noted that reviews generated by fellow consumers had a greater influence than those generated by professionals.

The report went on to say that, "ComScore asked the study participants how much they would be willing to pay for a particular service based on the quality of the service. The results showed that consumers were willing to pay between **20 percent and 99 percent more** for an Excellent (5 star) rating than for a Good (4 star rating), depending on the product category."

This underscores the need in the service industry not just to give good service (which is expected by the consumer), but to give outstanding service that is regarded as "remarkable" by the consumer. This then becomes part of the purchase "bragging rights," whereby the consumer creates "buzz" about the purchase to others, not only about the product but also about the service that went along with it.

To support this hypothesis that consumer-generated reviews really do affect buying behavior, a 2007 study by Deloitte & Touche USA reported that, "almost two-thirds (62%) of the respondents to an online poll said they now read online product reviews written by other consumers.

More than eight in 10 (82%) of those who read reviews said that their purchasing decisions have been directly influenced by those reviews. People have used the reviews both to confirm initial buying decisions and to change them."

While the percentages were slightly higher for younger shoppers, all age groups are reading and acting on online reviews, according to Deloitte. In addition, 69% of the respondents said they have shared online reviews with friends, family, or colleagues, the report stated.

What about negative reviews? Even the best brands will receive negative reviews at some point. According to a study by Euro RSCG Worldwide (http://www.eurorscg.com/flash/#/), 20% of consumers reportedly lash out at or about companies or their brands, due to the anonymity of social media. That leaves 80% of consumers who do not. In other words, 20% makes up those who are unhappy with your products or services; if you only have 10 unhappy customers out of the 1,000 you serve, then less than one percent of your customer base is likely to lash out.

Ignoring negative comments is foolish, and it only feeds the problem. Respond, and respond immediately. Inspect the problem being reported, fix it if it exists, and report back, keeping the dissatisfied consumer in the loop all the way.

Sadly, today we do not teach new employees to "complete the loop." Completing the loop simply means whoever you pass the negative comment to, YOU never negate contacting the complainer back yourself and keeping that customer in the loop every step of the way. You cannot overkill communications to satisfy a customer and all of their followers on the consumer review site.

7: Summary

Thank you for reading this book on social media marketing success. Here are 18 key points found in the book:

1. Social Media has been adopted so quickly by the public partly due to the need for Social Validation: "Social validation, or social proofing, is a psychological phenomenon that occurs in ambiguous situations when people do not have enough information to make opinions independently and instead look for external clues like popularity, third party endorsements, to friends and family to develop that level of trust." Wikipedia

2. What can we learn from social media that can be spread across all other areas of marketing? What can we learn to make our customer's experience more enjoyable, our product or service more accessible and, ultimately, more sales oriented?" Chris Brogan, http://www.chrisbrogan.com

3. Ask yourself **why** before you go into social media in a big way. Just because the technology exists does not mean you have to use it. I expect your business or organization has been

getting along quite well without social media. Before you go any further, answer the question, why am I getting into social media and adding more work?

4. Public relations are the development of social, political, and market capital through third party endorsements. The value of Public relations lies in capturing and reproducing it so it lives forever! -John Hope-Johnstone, *How to Market Tourism in the 21st Century.*

5. What is social media? Social media is the content; it's the writing, pictures, reviews, or videos that are placed on the Internet for interactive purposes. "Media is the intersection between technology and content." (Robert Iger, CEO Disney Corp.)

6. What is social networking? Social networking via the Internet is the connection that happens between people reading and viewing social media. The world famous sales guru Zig Ziglar once said, "Networking is getting what YOU want by helping other people get what THEY want." I have always held this to be true and it has never let me down.

7. Social Media provides a sort of "Ambient Intimacy" which is being able to keep in touch with people with a level of regularity and intimacy that you wouldn't usually have access to, because time and space conspire to make it impossible. Flickr lets me see what friends are eating for lunch, how they have redecorated their bedroom, their latest haircut. Twitter tells me when they are hungry, what technology is currently frustrating them, who they are having drinks with tonight.

8. Social media is NOT an answer; it is an enabler. It enables communities of common interest to find each other and have a conversation. Social media can be a great enabler for corporations to show their human face and to be transparent.

If that is deemed to be of value to the organization then it should be used; if it's not, then leave it alone. www.buzzmaster.wordpress.com, and slightly altered and expanded from Robert Abate's http://www.information-management.com/blog/robert_abate.htmlInformation Management blog, June 8, 2009.

9. Your presence has more to do with good content than your marketing pitch. Mitch Joel: http://www.twistimage.com/blog/archives/the-new-marketing-conversation/:

10. "Facebook is a Web 3.0 platform with the whole package. It straddles the Social Media and Social Networking divide perfectly." Hence, its dominance in the field. (Quoted from: http://lonscohen.com/blog/2009/04/difference-between-social-media-and-social-networking/)

11. Don't forget that blasting a message out just once is never going to reach all your social media followers. Do it at least five times over a week at different times of the day and with different wording but the same basic message and URL.

12. "A community is fundamentally an interdependent human system given form by the conversation it holds within itself." (Peter Block, *Community: The Structure of Belonging,* 2008. http://www.amazon.com/Community-Structure-Belonging-Peter-Block/dp/1576754871)

13. Two key elements to building your social media communities often forgotten are: 1) Build it with people who are key influencers in your world; and 2) Be social: Introduce people, mentor people, and help people get where they want to go. By doing this, you will build your own reputation and your community will prosper.

14. The first rule to improving your social media marketing is an understanding that each platform needs to cross promote. No platform stands alone. They all must eventually drive the participant to your Web site and a greater understanding of your brand.

15. Once you have notified all your "friends" about your new fan page, email list, Twitter followers and exhausted every other avenue of contact, then it is time to get serious. NOTHING will grow your "fans" on facebook faster than a good offer and a Google AdWords advertising campaign. For a few dollars every month you will provide continual growth for the Facebook fan page.

16. Author Mark Hughes defines buzz as "capturing the attention of consumers and the media to the point where talking about your brand or destination becomes entertaining, fascinating and newsworthy." (*Buzzmarketing: Get People to Talk About Your Stuff*, 2008.
http://www.buzzmarketing.com/about.html)

17. What is a hook? It is the essence of your story, the angle, the concept that can be boiled down to a few words. In a way, your hook is the bait, like a headline that makes someone want to read the whole story.

18. The power of long tail keywords is best explained by the Key Effectiveness Indicator (KEI). Web CEO, (a free download, http://www.webceo.com/), has coined the phrase "Key Effectiveness Indicator". A Key Effectiveness Indicator is a mathematical formula of the relationship between the number of Web sites that respond to a search term and the actual number of searches over a given period of time.

I hope there are many more take-aways you have found in this book in addition to the above 18 points. Please contact me if you have any questions or comments. johnhopejohnstone@gmail.com

8: Appendix

Here are URLs that will help you measure and monitor your social media strategy.

1. Brand Monitoring:

HowSociable? – A simple, free, tool that can measure the visibility of your brand on the web across 22 metrics. (http://www.howsociable.com/)

Addict-o-matic – A nice search engine that aggregates RSS feeds, allows you to quickly see the areas where a brand is lacking in presence. (http://addictomatic.com/)

Social Mention – A social media search engine offering searches across individual platforms (blogs, microblogs) or all, together with a 'social rank' score. Whether or not the score is transparent enough to be meaningful is open to debate. (http://socialmention.com/)

2. Macroblog Monitoring:

TECHNORATI Search – Technorati's new search interface. Use it to find top blogs based upon inbound links only. (http://technorati.com/search/)

TECHNORATI Advanced – Technorati's advanced search page allows you to search for blogs (rather than articles) based on tags. (http://technorati.com/search?advanced)

Google Blog Search – Google's index of blog articles. The advanced search tab allows you to search based on additional criteria. (http://blogsearch.google.com/)

IceRocket – Blog search tool that also graphs! (http://www.icerocket.com/)

BlogPulse – Search for blog articles by keyword. Developed by Nielsen BuzzMetrics. (http://www.blogpulse.com/)

3. Microblog Monitoring:

Digg – Social bookmarking, mainly for news, images and videos. (http://digg.com/)

StumbleUpon – Social bookmarking – general cool stuff. (http://www.stumbleupon.com/)

Del.icio.us – Social bookmarking. (http://www.delicious.com/)

Twitter Search – Search keywords on Twitter, which "self-refreshes". See what's happening — 'right now'. (http://search.twitter.com/)

Twitter Advanced Search - I use this a great deal for finding tweets that are asking for help in social media. Hence, I make new friends. (http://search.twitter.com/advanced)

Twitstat – Twitter Tweitgeist – Tag cloud for last 500 Tweets. (http://www.twitstat.com/cloud.html)

Tweet Scan – search for words on Twitter. (http://tweetscan.com/)

Twitturly – see what people are talking about on Twitter. (http://twitturly.com/)

Hash tags – Real-time tracking of Twitter hash tags. (http://hashtags.org/)

TweetBeep – Track mentions of your brand on Twitter in real time. (http://tweetbeep.com/)

Twitrratr – Rates mentions of your search term on Twitter as positive/neutral/negative. (http://twitrratr.com/)

TweetMeme – View the most popular Twitter threads occurring now. (http://tweetmeme.com/)

Twitscoop – Through an automated algorithm, Twitscoop crawls hundreds of tweets every minute, extracts the words mentioned more often than usual, and creates a tag cloud. (http://www.twitscoop.com/)

Friend or Follower - Find out who you are following that's not following you, a useful growth monitor on Twitter. (http://landing.domainsponsor.com/?a_id=1375&adultfilter=off&pop under=off&domainname=friendorfollower.com)

Klout.com- Will rank your Twitter presence in a quadrant to show where you are. (http://klout.com/)

4. Buzz Monitoring:

Google Trends – shows amount of searches and Google news stories. (http://google.com/trends)

Trendpedia – Create charts showing the volume of discussion around multiple topics. Generates cool graphs. (http://www.trendpedia.com/)

BlogPulse Trends – Compare the mentions of specific keywords and phrases in blog articles. (http://blogpulse.com/trend)

Omgili charts – Omgili Buzz Graphs let you measure and compare the Buzz of any term, mostly from review sites/forums. (http://omgili.com/graphs.html)

eKstreme – blog data is obtained from Technorati and the social bookmarks come from del.icio.us. (http://ekstreme.com/buzz)

5. Message Board Monitoring:

BoardTracker – tracks words in forums.
(http://www.boardtracker.com/)

BoardReader – Search multiple message boards and forums.
(http://boardreader.com/)

Omgili – Omgili is a specialized search engine that focuses on "many to many" user generated content platforms, such as, forums, discussion groups, mailing lists, answer boards and others. Omgili finds consumer opinions, debates, discussions, personal experiences, answers and solutions. (http://omgili.com/)

Google Groups – Searches usenet groups.
(http://groups.google.com/?pli=1)

Yahoo! Groups – Searches all Yahoo! Groups.
(http://groups.yahoo.com/)

6. Trend Monitoring:

Google Trends – Search trends and see search volume by country and region. (http://www.google.com/trends)

Wordtracker Keywords – Displays average daily search volume of a given keyword or phrase. (http://freekeywords.wordtracker.com/)

Google Keyword Tool – Generate keyword ideas for related keywords and search volumes.
(https://adwords.google.com/o/Targeting/Explorer?__u=1000000000 &__c=1000000000&ideaRequestType=KEYWORD_IDEAS#search.none)

Web CEO – Keyword tracking, SEO tool and charting search phrase usage by month. (http://www.webceo.com/)

7. Multimedia Search:

Metacafe – A High-traffic video search engine.
(http://www.metacafe.com/)

Google Advanced Video Search – Search for videos.
(http://video.google.com/videoadvancedsearch)

Truveo – Aggregate video search engine. Search videos from YouTube,
MySpace, and AOL. (http://www.truveo.com/)

Viral Video Chart – Displays top 20 most-viewed video (1, 7, 365 days).
Includes view counts and charting.
(http://viralvideochart.unrulymedia.com/)

Guardian's Viral Video Chart – Weekly roundup of what's excellent on
the Web.
(http://www.guardian.co.uk/technology/series/viralvideochart)

8. Feed Aggregator:

Yahoo Pipes – Feed aggregator and manipulator. Set up pipes for news
alerts and overviews. (http://pipes.yahoo.com/pipes/)